精神

[Seishin / Say-sheen]
This is the ideogram for spirit;
the defining essence of
the character of the
Japanese

The special character and ability of the Japanese were recognized by more astute Western visitors even before Japan's feudal age ended. American ship captain Henry Holmes, who made a number of trips to Japan prior to the opening of the country to the West in 1853 noted in his journal: "They [the Japanese] will surprise the world!"
—*KATA: The Key to Understanding & Dealing with the Japanese!*—

Why the Japanese Are a Superior People!

The Advantage of Using Both Sides of Your Brain!

Boyé Lafayette De Mente

Copyright © 2009 by Boyé Lafayette De Mente.
All rights reserved.

PHOENIX BOOKS / PUBLISHERS
ISBN: 978-0914778-55-2

ACKNOWLEDGEMENTS

I am deeply indebted to the following people for decades of friendship, goodwill and support:

Prof. Michihiro Matsumoto
Whose career has included martial artist, simultaneous interpreter, corporate executive, NHK TV host, author of over one hundred books, debate society founder-president and leader of the Inter-Cultural English Exchange.

Prof. Mutsuo Shukuya
Educator, tanka poet master, author, newspaper columnist, book reviewer, cultural advisor and advocate of spreading the writing of tanka and haiku poetry around the world.

Tokuo (Paul) Maruoka
International banker, business consultant, corporate executive and corporate advisor—with whose family I lived while attending Jōchi Daigaku [Sophia University] in Tokyo in the early 1950s when he was a teenager.

Dr. Tadanobu Tsunoda
Japan's leading authority on speech and hearing and author of the seminal book *The Japanese Mind*, in which he states that the Japanese are primarily right-brain oriented because of their language—a factor that gives them many advantages.
I was one of his lab subjects.

Yoshio Karita
Formerly Ministry of Foreign Affairs official and chief of protocol for the Imperial Household, then Senior Advisor to the Mori Building Co… and strong supporter of my efforts to break down cultural barriers between Japan and the world at large.

Other Books by the Author

Japanese Etiquette & Ethics in Business
Korean Etiquette & Ethics in Business
Chinese Etiquette & Ethics in Business
Chinese in Plain English
Korean in Plain English
Japanese in Plain English
Instant Japanese / Survival Japanese
Instant Korean / Survival Korean
Instant Chinese / Survival Chinese
Japan Made Easy—All You Need to Know to Enjoy Japan
Dining Guide to Japan / Shopping Guide to Japan
Etiquette Guide to Japan
Etiquette Guide to China
Etiquette Guide to Korea
Business Guide to Japan
Japan's Cultural Code Words
China's Cultural Code Words
Mexican Cultural Code Words
The Japanese Have a Word for It!
Subway Guide to Tokyo
Korea's Business & Cultural Code Words
There is a Word for It in Mexico
The Sensual Side of the Orient
KATA—The Key to Understanding & Dealing
with the Japanese)
Asian Face Reading—Unlocking the Secrets
Hidden in the Human Face

The Japanese Samurai Code—Classic Strategies for Success

Which Side of Your Brain am I Talking To?—The Advantages of Using Both Sides of Your Brain

People-Sexing—How to Measure the Sexuality of Men & Women by their Facial Features

Romantic Hawaii—Sun, Sand, Surf & Sex

Romantic Mexico—The Image & the Realities

Why Mexicans Think and Behave the Way They Do!—The Cultural Factors that Created the Character & Personality of the Mexican People

Samurai Principles and Practices that Will Help Preteens & Teens in School, Sports, Social Activities & Choosing Careers

Japan Unmasked—The Character & Culture of the Japanese

Elements of Japanese Design—Understanding and Using Japan's Classic *Wabi-Sabi-Shibui* Concepts

Sex and the Japanese—The Sensual Side of Japan

Samurai Strtegies—42 Secret Martial Arts from Musashi's "Book of Five Rings"

The Myth of Intelligent Life on Planet Earth

The Chinese Mind—Understanding Traditional Chinese Beliefs and Their Influence on Contemporary Culture

ONCE A FOOL—From Japan to Alaska by Amphibious Jeep

*Various titles published in Chinese, Croatian, Czech, French, German, Hebrew, Italian, Indonesian, Japanese, Polish, Russian and Spanish.

*

The Spiritual Drive of the Japanese

One of the most important factors in the prowess and accomplishments of the Japanese is that historically their culture imbued them with a condition known as *Ki ga sumanai* [Kee gah suu-mah-nie], which means something like "My spirit is not satisfied!"
In other words, the Japanese have been culturally programmed to be dissatisfied with any thought, action or product that is less than perfect...

*

*

The Japanese Sense of Self

The Japanese have a powerful sense of self that includes exceptional pride in their national identity, and see themselves in competition with the rest of the world, not only economically but culturally as well—a factor that motivates them to go to extraordinary lengths to validate their self image.

*

CONTENTS

Preface

Which Side of Your Brain Am I Talking To?

Cross-Over between Brains

Male & Female Differences

Cultural Differences

[1] The Japanese Language Factor

[2] Right-Brained Japan

[3] The Impact of Right-Brain Dominance On Japanese Culture

[4] Fuzzy Thinking vs. Linear Thinking

[5]
Emotions vs. Reason

[6]
Intuition vs. Reason

[7]
Etiquette vs. Disharmony

[8]
Policies vs. Principles

[9]
Aestheticism vs. Practicality

[10]
Conformism vs. Entrepreneurship

[11]
Femininity vs. Masculinity

[12]
Humanism vs. Scientism

[13]
Groupism vs. Individualism

[14]
Harmony vs. Reality

[15]
Passivity vs. Aggression

[16]
Spirit vs. Reality

[17]
Quality vs. Profit

[18]
Diligence vs. Getting By

[19]
Risk-Aversion vs. Risk-Taking

[20]
Sincerity vs. Insincerity

[21]
Wet vs. Dry

[22]
Right-Brain Views
That Distinguish the Japanese

Aesthetics
Apparel
Art

Beauty
Bathing
Business Management
Bragging
Cuteness
Decision-Making
Etiquette
Flattery
Humility
Intelligence
Mental Health
Problem Solving
Self-Respect
Sex
Shame
Spirituality
Style

Preface

Which Side of Your Brain Am I Talking To?

It has been proven beyond reasonable doubt that there are basic differences in the functioning and roles of the left and right sides of the brain.

Scientists tell us that the left sphere of the brain is programmed for linear or straight-line thinking, and is "in charge" of routine, repetitive physical actions, for the use of logic, for direct verbal communication, and for making objective, fact-based decisions, etc.

The right side of the brain, on the other hand, is said to be more concerned with emotions, intuitions, personal relations, aesthetics, mutual cooperation, group orientation, and maintaining harmony through nonverbal communication and indirect speech.

Cross-Over between Brains

Obviously, there is considerable cross-over between the two sides of the brain, but the basic functions of its two sides are different, resulting in people reacting differently, depending on which side of the brain is engaged.

In *left-brain* cultures the right side of the brain is engaged when contemplating and discussing matters of religion, aesthetics, and other esoteric subjects not based on hard, objective facts...and this, of course, is why such discussions tend to become very emotional.

Interestingly, however, some people in essentially right-brain cultures are capable of putting on left-brain thinking caps when pursuing practical matters such as engineering, math and scientific research. And in that case, they are often able to benefit from using both sides of their brains in tandem...a process that I call holistic thinking.

Male & Female Differences

There is also a significant difference in the basic brain orientation of men and women. In predominately *left-brain* oriented cultures women tend to be *right-brained* in their thinking and behavior. Their attitudes and behavior have a higher emotional and intuitive content than that of men. They are more caring, more nurturing and more aesthetically inclined than men.

In predominately *right-brain* cultures, women tend to be *less* right-brain oriented than the men. While they are more caring and nurturing than men they are typically also more direct and more practical in their attitudes and behavior as a survival trait.

Cultural Differences

Some cultures are left-brain oriented, and others are right-brain oriented. Among the left-brain oriented cultures, the most prominent include China, the United States, Germany, England, Russia and Israel. The cultures of all Spanish speaking countries, as well as France and Italy, are combinations of left-brain and right-brain thinking and behavior.

According to a prominent Japanese authority on the brain, Dr. Tadanobu Tsunoda, the two most right-brain oriented cultures on the planet are those of Japan and the Polynesian speaking nations of the South Pacific.

There is, in fact, ample evidence that the right-brain orientation of the Japanese is the main source of many of their most positive cultural traits, and played a major role in their being able to transform their tiny, resource-poor war-devastated country into an economic superpower in less than 30 years.

Boyé Lafayette De Mente

*

The Power of Beauty

One of the secrets of Japan's commercial prowess is
its cultural emphasis on aesthetics. Very early in their
history the Japanese developed an acute awareness of
the beauty in nature, leading them to incorporate this
awareness into their arts and crafts and to devise
rituals to make the same standards of beauty
an integral part of their daily lives.
—*KATA: The Key to Understanding & Dealing with
the Japanese*—

WHY THE JAPANESE ARE A SUPERIOR PEOPLE!

The Japanese Language Factor

Japan's Dr. Tadanobu Tsunoda, noted author of *The Japanese Brain* and other books who began as an audiologist and otologist, learned during decades of research that there is a fundamental difference in the hemispheric dominance in the brains of Japanese and non-Japanese. The Japanese process certain sounds and information in the *right* sides of their brains, and non-Japanese process certain sounds and information in the *left* sides of their brains—and they are not always the same.

Further research by Dr. Tsunoda demonstrated that this difference in brain dominance is a direct result of the native language of each individual. What was even more remarkable is that he found that there were only two languages that *always* produce right-brain dominance in people: Japanese and Polynesian.

Dr. Tsunoda learned that the secret of which side of the brain is used to process sounds was based on whether or not the sounds were harmonic or non-harmonic.

More research revealed that Japanese and Polynesian are harmonic languages and are therefore processed by the right side of the brain, while all other languages are non-harmonic and are therefore processed by the left side of the brain.

The vowel sounds A (ah), I (ee), U (uu), E (eh) and O (oh), predominate in Japanese and Polynesian, making them "harmonic languages."

Dr. Tsunoda also reaffirmed that the left side of the brain is dominate in logic and calculation, and the right side of the brain is dominate in the expression of emotions, music, the recognition of shapes, responding to natural sounds, and thought processes pertaining to analogy.

In another surprise, Dr. Tsunoda found that the sounds produced by Western musical instruments are processed by the *right side* of the brain, and sounds produced by Japanese musical instruments are processed by the *left side* of the brain.

On the surface, this might appear to be a contradiction, but the answer lies in the fact that music produced by Japanese instruments is non-harmonic, while that produced by Western instruments is harmonic—reinforcing Dr. Tsunoda's findings that the left side of the brain processes non-harmonic sounds, while the right side of the brain processes harmonic sounds.

In his experiments, Dr. Tsunoda learned that the switching between the two brain hemispheres occurs primarily in the brain stem, located under the cortex, which divides the brain into the harmonic brain (the right side), where harmonious Western music is processed, and the non-harmonic brain (the left side), which non-harmonious Japanese music is processed.

He also determined that this switching process is hard-wired into the brain by the time an individual is eight or nine years old as a direct result of exposure to speech sounds, and that consonants in speech syllables are automatically switched to the left side of the brain, while vowel-dominate syllables are switched to the right side of the brain. He says that the switching of sounds appears to be related to their frequencies as measured in hertz.

Another interesting result of his experiments was that sexual functions appear to be processed by the right side of the brain in left-brain oriented people—the opposite of what he expected. The answer, he postulates, is that sexual behavior is so laden with emotion that it becomes a right-brain function.

Dr. Tsunoda's experiments proved that the difference between Japanese and non-Japanese in brain dominance is purely environmental, and not related to race in any way. He tested Japanese-Americans who had been raised in the U.S., and found that like other non-Japanese they processed emotions on the right side of their brains, and English on the left side of their brains.

Another of the more intriguing results suggested by Dr. Tsunoda's research is that cosmic activity, the rotation of the earth and lunar motion, etc., appears to have an influence on the switching between the left and right sides of the brain.

He says this suggests a sub-cortical biological function that could go back to the earliest days when mankind was much closer to nature and could probably feel the connection with the earth and the cosmos, as birds and animals appear to do.

The Influence of Kanji on the Japanese

Many of the attributes of the Japanese that contributed to their prowess now and in centuries past were a result of their learning and using the ancient Chinese ideographic system of writing—called *Hanzi* [Hahn-jee] in Chinese and *Kanji* [Kahn-jee] in Japanese.

In addition to making the Japanese good at doing small, complicated things with their hands and enhancing their sensitivity to forms and designs, training in memorizing and writing Kanji also conditioned them to be patient and to persevere in their goals.

The long-term use of ideograms thus became a mold that shaped the Japanese physically, emotionally and intellectually, homogenizing them and binding them to their culture.

[2]

Right-Brained Japan

As the world's only large, prominent, group of people whose mindset is primarily right-brained the Japanese are both unique and in a unique position. Their right-brain orientation is the primary source of their most attractive and positive cultural traits, as well as traits that are negative and often seriously disadvantageous when they interact with left-brain oriented people.

One of the most positive cultural traits that the Japanese have inherited from the influence of their language is the ability to apply both right and left-brain insight and energy in all of their efforts. One of the most negative elements that derives from the extraordinary emotional content of Japanese culture is that it makes it difficult and time-consuming for them to maintain harmonious relationships—especially with people whose cultures are less emotion laden.

The government-sponsored industrialization of Japan between 1870 and 1890 required left-brain decision-making and a growing degree of left-brain behavior at the expense of the country's traditional right-brain culture. The introduction of democracy into

Japan by the United States in 1945-6, and by the ongoing massive importation of popular American culture since then, further eroded the day-to-day role of its right-brain mindset.

But this erosion process did not penetrate to the core of the culture or psyche of the Japanese because the Japanese language remained virtually intact, and continued to program them in the right-brain mode.

While this right-brain programming process continues today it is mitigated somewhat by the exposure of a large percentage of the population to the English language, first as students, and then as adults in many of their activities. The more English that is imprinted on the left side of their brains, the more the Japanese can deliberately and readily switch to left-brain thinking and acting.

This process does not "delete" their right-brain programming, but it effectively over-rides it as long as they are thinking and conversing in English. However, making the shift from right-brain Japanese to left-brain English is not effortless. Not being used to processing language with the left side of their brains, speaking and listening to English can be tiring, especially if they are not very good at the language.

Naturally enough, until the English-speaking Japanese achieves a certain level of fluency it does not "feel" right, and in some instances, in business and other areas, what is said in English is not regarded as official or binding.

For the foreseeable future, the core of Japanese culture is going to remain right-brained, which, as it turns out in the increasingly global world, is an advantage. One of the elements that is a definite plus is that the Japanese automatically bring a holistic approach to their research and design efforts. One of the factors that is definitely a minus is that they continue to have difficulty interacting effectively with people from left-brain cultures.

There is a positive side to the Japanese being required to learn English—if they begin the study in early childhood. Brain research indicates that people who are bilingual from a young age are less likely to suffer age-related mental decline as they get older.

The scientists say this beneficial effect probably results from the fact that the brain has to work harder to handle two (or more!) languages, and this exercise keeps its neural pathways in better shape.

*

Fury in the Work Place

Another cultural characteristic of the Japanese that contributed enormously to their success in becoming an economic superpower in less than 30 years is incorporated in the phrase *moretsu shain* [moe-rate-suu shah-een], which is usually translated as "gung-ho employee / employees."
The cultural implication of *moretsu shain* becomes much clearer when you consider that the word *moretsu* literally means "fury" or "violence"—and that when used in the above context it refers to the traditional custom or habit of the Japanese to work hard for long hours—a custom that has virtually disappeared among the younger generations and does not bode well for the future of Japan.

[3]
The Impact of Right-Brain Dominance On Japanese Culture

Right-brain dominance in Japanese culture has been profound, influencing every aspect of their deepest values, their motivations, and their day-to-day thinking and behavior. This influence is especially visible in their arts and crafts and in everything else that is normally described as being *Japanese*, including in the way they go about such mundane things as arranging food on a plate.

The role and influence of these physical manifestations of the right-brain dominance in Japanese culture are positive, and account for virtually all of the things that both Japanese and non-Japanese find so attractive and so emotionally and spiritually satisfying.

Interestingly [but not surprisingly to old Japan hands], the manifestations that Japan's right-brain dominant culture elicits from viewers is primarily sensual. When people who are aesthetically attuned view these tangible things they experience a variety of pleasant feelings that are sexual in nature.

In all of the other areas of Japanese life that involve intangible facets of the culture, everything that comes under the heading of attitudes and behavior is directly and immediately impacted by the right-brain orientation of the Japanese—and this impact is frequently negative.

When the Japanese are dealing with other Japanese and all are on the same cultural channel, the aspects of their right-brain orientation that conflict with characteristic left-brain attitudes and behavior are generally kept under control by a variety of institutionalized forms of communication, tolerance, and cooperation.

By the same token, when the Japanese are dealing with people whose left-brains are dominate and who have not been culturally programmed to accommodate right-brain thinking and behavior, misunderstandings and some measure of friction are inevitable—especially when the left-brain people concerned are not sensitive to cultural differences or choose to ignore them.

Since the late 1800s, many Japanese have been forced to become acutely aware that their values and behavior often differ markedly from those of foreigners—especially Westerners—but just knowing that the differences exist does not mean that they are easy to overcome, especially when both sides have been programmed to believe that their way is the best way.

In most of their international dealings, the Japanese have been forced to be the first and sometimes the only ones to alter their way of doing things in order to succeed in business and political affairs.

The line between right-brain thinking and behaving and left-brain thinking and behaving is not always clear, and cross-thinking and behaving is common. However, in many areas of business, professional and social relationships these differences are pronounced enough that they can be quantified, making it possible for people who are aware of them to adjust their thinking and behavior to accommodate the differences.

The following chapters cover some key areas in which the typical right-brain approach of the Japanese generally contrasts sharply with the left-brain approach of non-Japanese, and more often than not, ends up being an advantage for the Japanese.

WHY THE JAPANESE ARE A SUPERIOR PEOPLE!

Understanding by Observing

During the 1970s and 80s when foreign businesspeople came to Tokyo and asked me to help them understand why and how the Japanese could be so successful in virtually every aspect of business, I took them to a leading department store when it first opened in the morning and let them observe the manners and actions of the employees. After about thirty minutes of intently watching what went on in the store they invariably turned to me and said:
"Now I understand!"

*

[4]

Fuzzy Thinking vs. Linear Thinking

The "mother" factor in the Japanese way of thinking is what I call "fuzzy thinking," or "holistic thinking," which often contrasts sharply with the linear way most of the rest of the world thinks.

This supposition is based in part on the observable way the Japanese think and behave, and in part on the theory of Dr. Tadanobu Tsunoda, which proposes that the right side of the brain is dominant in the Japanese, as opposed to left-brain dominance in non-Japanese—a circumstance that makes the Japanese virtually unique in the world, despite their cultural kinship with Koreans and Chinese.

While there are a number of similarities in the traditional cultures of the Japanese, Koreans and Chinese, these similarities came about because primitive Korea and then primitive Japan adopted many facets of Chinese culture very early in their histories.

And while these cultural imports from China included virtually all of the arts and crafts that came to be associated with Korea and Japan, along with the very sophisticated Chinese way of writing as well as the form of government, Buddhism, Confucianism and Taoism, both Korea and Japan retained their own native cultural essence that makes them conspicuously different from the Chinese.

In the case of Japan, the cultural factor that made the Japanese different in the first place and prevented them from becoming total clones of the Chinese, was, according to Dr. Tsunoda's theory, the nature of the Japanese language, which made the right side of their brains dominant.

While there are some who dispute Dr. Tsunoda's theory, there can be no disputing the proposition that the Japanese think and behave differently, because these differences can be both observed and deduced.

Even a cursory study of Japan's traditional culture, especially after the emergence of the samurai class from 1192, clearly demonstrates that the Japanese were perfectly capable of thinking in linear terms when it came to structuring and enforcing the new shogunate form of government.

But in implementing and maintaining this form of government, and in going about the daily affairs of living and working, the Japanese were significantly influenced by the dominance of the right side of their brains.

This right-brain influence was manifested in their approach to arts and crafts, in their architecture, in designing their gardens, in their emphasis on aesthetic practices, in their extraordinary attachment to poetry, and in their overall view of nature.

In fact, the dominance of the right side of their brains was so powerful that the Japanese had an aversion to thinking that was based solely on facts and logic. They regarded this way of thinking as callous, cruel and anti-human. The attribute they most admired in people was "humanism."

Contact with the left-brained oriented Western world, first in the mid-16th century and then again in the mid-1800s, was to have profound consequences for both. Japan's right-brain oriented culture clashed with the cultures of the West.

But there was early evidence that the holistic way of thinking that was more characteristic of the Japanese than it was of Westerners was going to give them a special advantage in the future.

One of the most telling demonstrations of this special advantage occurred when the U.S.'s Commodore Perry and his fleet of black warships arrived in Japan in 1853 to force the country to open its doors to the outside world.

Perry and his men went ashore at the tiny fishing village of Shimoda at the end of Izu Peninsula, well south of the Shogunate headquarters in Edo (Tokyo). Perry presented the samurai delegation of the local lord with a miniature train that was powered by steam. The Japanese had never seen a train before. They took it away and three days later came back with several suggestions for improving its technology.

WHY THE JAPANESE ARE A SUPERIOR PEOPLE!

Within a few decades the Japanese had demonstrated an extraordinary ability to understand, duplicate and improve on the technology of a wide range of Western imports. And despite some foreign views to the contrary, the Japanese were soon to prove that they were also capable of basic research leading to new technology.

Following the debacle of the Japanese attempt to conquer East Asia, Southeast Asia and the islands of the Pacific, their ability to absorb, improve on and innovate technology played a key role in their quick emergence as the second largest economy in the world—an absolutely incredible phenomenon that many Westerners still have difficulty understanding and accepting.

The natural tendency of the Japanese to look at all things from a holistic viewpoint continues to be a valuable asset, especially in the use of technology and aesthetic factors that do not directly threaten the entrenched bureaucracies of business and government.

There are, however, negative elements in the right-brain orientation of the Japanese that have continued to plague them, often making them feel and look like fish out of water. This includes an ongoing discomfort with unadorned logical thinking, quick decision-making, and dealing on a level playing field with left-brain thinkers.

However, the more experienced the Japanese become at cross-over thinking, the more the negative influences of their right-brain orientation will diminish, and the more they will gain from being able to view things holistically.

The Japanese are well aware of the fact that there is a fundamental difference in the way they think and the way others think, and this has resulted in them being virtually obsessed with these differences, turning the study and writing about them into a major industry. More than one theory has been advanced to explain these differences.

Rather than using the right-brain left-brain theory to explain these differences, Professor Michinobu Kato, author of *Watakushi-tachi no Nihonjin Ron*, or *Our Japanology*, and other works, describes the Japanese as analog thinkers and others as digital thinkers. He says that this is the reason the Japanese are not good at theory or abstract thinking…which has proven to be a false assumption.

Prof. Kato goes on to say that the Japanese are not good at dealing with matters of high finance and Western style management, suggesting that their digital thinking limits the depth and scope of their thinking. He adds, however, that the Japanese are exceptionally good at dealing with practical, concrete matters such as manufacturing and building things because they do not require logical debate.

The Making of the Japanese

The ultimate goal in traditional Japanese education among the samurai and professional classes was for the pupil to become one with the object of the training. The goal of the swordsman was to merge his consciousness with his sword; the painter with his brush; the potter with his clay; the garden designer with the materials of the garden. Once this was achieved, as the theory goes, the doing of a thing perfectly was as easy as thinking it.
—*KATA: The Key to Understanding & Dealing with the Japanese!*—

[5]
Emotions vs. Reason

Long before I had ever heard of Dr. Tadanobu Tsunoda's theory of the Japanese being primarily right-brain oriented, I had written extensively about the emotional content in the character of the Japanese and in their culture.

I noted in one of my earlier books that Westerners who go to Japan for business purposes, or take up residence there for any purpose, and come face-to-face with typical Japanese behavior are inevitably surprised and often frustrated by instances when emotion rather than reason determines the actions and reactions of the Japanese.

I also noted that nothing was more irritating to the logical-minded Westerner than becoming involved with anyone who does not behave in a "reasonable" manner—much less encountering a whole nation of "unreasonable" people.

As it turned out, however, the Japanese actually have a dual mindset made up of a combination of emotional intelligence and reasoning power. And when this dual mindset is brought to bear in combination, it gives them extra insight, which they call *kansei* (kahn-say-ee), or "emotional rightness" and use in reference to how people perceive, react to and use products. This term may also be translated as "absolute awareness," in which case it refers to the emotional and rational content of a product—and is an insight, or skill, that the Japanese have in abundance.

In addition to deliberately building *kansei* into their products, the Japanese also infuse it into their advertising campaigns, generally giving it more priority than the utilitarian value of the product.

The many wonderful aesthetic elements in Japan's traditional arts and crafts are among the positive manifestations of the emotional orientation of the people. The traditional human-centered "emotional" approach to business management was a rational and humane way of doing things, and it worked exceedingly well until Western style competition, internationally as well as domestically, made it disadvantageous.

Now that Japan has become dependent upon foreign economic and political relationships with people who are left-brain oriented, the emotional factor in their makeup can be a serious handicap or an advantage, depending on their awareness of the factor, their experience in using it, or in suppressing it.

Their relationships with less emotional people can be even more complicated based on the reaction of the foreign side. Some non-Japanese are better able to manage emotional factors than others. Many Americans in particularly appear to have no insights or skills in dealing with emotional situations.

Up to this time, most of the burden of dealing with the emotional content the Japanese bring to foreign business relationships has been placed on their shoulders by default. As in other areas of their culture that are different from or incompatible with others, those involved in international affairs are becoming more experienced and more skilled in managing the emotional factors, and in assuming a purely rational approach.

In keeping with Dr. Tsunoda's theory that English is processed on the left side of the brain, which is the "logical" side, those Japanese who have learned enough English to express themselves fairly well seem to be able to suppress the "emotional conditioning" of their native tongue and speak without the ambiguity that is built into the language.

However, this facility in English frequently results in problems developing afterward. The foreign listener naturally takes the speaker at his or her word—his or her *English* word, that is—only to discover later that this assumption is misplaced.

It often happens in business, diplomatic and other situations that Japanese will make statements and/or commitments in English that either do not reflect their real positions, or are not acceptable by the group or organization they represent.

Whether or not these statements and positions by individuals speaking in English are meant to be devious or deceitful, or merely express what the Japanese believes the foreign listener wants to hear without any intention of doing harm, depends on the situation.

WHY THE JAPANESE ARE A SUPERIOR PEOPLE!

The Japanese are very experienced at dealing with ambiguous speech that can be take in different ways, since it is a characteristic of the Japanese language and a key factor in their intellectual conditioning. They naturally leave it up to the other party to divine what they really mean or the nature of the real situation.

This cultural habit may carry over into their use of English or other foreign languages, since there is the built-in mindset that what they say directly is *tatemae* (tah-tay-my), or a façade to draw the other person out and maintain harmony; not their *honne* (hoan-nay), their real thoughts or intentions.

In other words, the right-brained derived emotional content in the character of the Japanese is not the only factor that influences their attitudes and behavior. The influence of the ambiguity of the Japanese language, which is built into the language to help ensure harmony in all relationships, also plays an important role in their day-to-day relationships with other Japanese as well as non-Japanese.

Here too, the Japanese tendency to combine emotion with reason often turns out to be an advantage in their relationships with non-Japanese, because no matter how logic-oriented the other side may be, there is a part of them that wants and responds positively to the human (emotional) touch.

[6]

Intuition vs. Reason

One of the most important of the cultural traits that the Japanese derived from their right-brain orientation was the practice of giving intuition precedence over reason, especially in very weighty affairs when the consequences were or could be enormous.

Japanese history is replete with incidents in which the fate of individuals, groups and even the nation itself hung in the balance, and the decisions made were based on intuition rather than reason. In fact, the higher placed and more powerful the individuals concerned in these situations, the more likely they were to depend on intuition rather than reason.

Stories about leading samurai of old and leading businessmen of the recent past, including the great Konosuke Matsushita, invariably include tales of their use of intuition as their primary source of wisdom, and in the decisions they made.

There is a special word in the Japanese language that refers to this kind of decision-making. It is called *haragei* (hah-rah-gay-ee), which literally translates as "the art of the stomach"—a more elegant phrase than the Western "gut feeling."

What *haragei* refers to is the use of common cultural knowledge to make decisions that are compatible with the mindset and spirit of the Japanese, and will therefore be accepted and acted on in the manner desired.

Haragei therefore equates to some extent with what I call "cultural telepathy"—that is, being able to communicate with people on the basis of common knowledge and common experience; although there is another, precise, word for this form of resolving situations and making decisions: *chokkan* (choke-kahn), which translates as "intuition."

The reason why intuition has traditionally played such an important role in Japanese life is because the people were homogenized to an extraordinary degree by their programming in exactly the same beliefs and forms of behavior, and therefore thought and acted very much alike.

This meant that they could intuit what others were thinking and what they would probably do under most circumstances. It also meant that they "knew" what was right and wrong without having to resort to reasoning it out, because the "correct" opinion or reaction was common knowledge.

Present-day Japanese are far less homogenous than what they were as late as the 1970s and 80s, but the power of the traditional culture is still very much in evidence in the attitudes and behavior of older people, and most of the time it is still possible to assume that in group situations they will react in "the Japanese way"—that is, according to identifiable Japanese values that remain traditional to varying degrees.

One of the challenges in dealing effectively with Japanese in situations where the individual is a member of a group is being able to determine whether a reaction is based on intuition or reason. Among younger individuals reason now generally overrides intuition except in group situations.

Generally, reactions that are based on intuition reflect the traditional Japanese mindset as a whole, while reactions based on pure reason may reflect the opinion or position of individuals, and not be binding on the group.

There is a great deal of "folk wisdom" in "Japanese intuition," and when that is combined with reason, it often results in a more comprehensive answer or solution to whatever discussion or problem is at hand.

*

Business as a Religion

Some decades after the beginning of the Tokugawa Shogunate, which ruled Japan from 1603 to 1868, a would-be businessman began promoting the concept that business should be regarded as and treated as a religion—that such an approach was far superior to the profit motive.

This business-as-a religion advocate began to preach his theory in the streets of Kyoto. After he began attracting large audiences he moved his preaching to halls that would accommodate them.

As time passed the concept of business as a religion gradually permeated the mindset of most Japanese businesspeople on all levels, from shopkeepers to owners of large-scale companies.

This concept was conspicuously present in the management approach of most of Japan's first generation of entrepreneurs following the fall of the Tokugawa government in 1867/68, and continues to be discernible in most companies in Japan today.

*

[7]
Etiquette vs. Disharmony

The Japanese regard Americans as the most unpredictable people on the planet because we do not have a precise etiquette that everyone follows in speech or in physical behavior.

In contrast, to our individualistic way of talking and behaving, the Japanese have traditionally behaved according to a strict, prescribed, uniform etiquette that was equated with morality and being civilized, and was perfectly predictable.

Japanese etiquette grew out of ritualistic behavior that was designed to show respect toward all of the spirits of nature, and was then refined and institutionalized in their daily lives by the influence of Confucian precepts that were imported from China.

The goal of Japanese etiquette was to ensure harmony, not only between them and the many gods of their pantheon, but among themselves—harmony that came to be based on absolute respect for parents, seniors, teachers, and those in positions of power.

This respect-etiquette system that developed in Japan was influenced in very specific and powerful ways by the right-brain character of the people, which made them nature-oriented, harmony-oriented and emotionally compulsive about doing things in an orderly, ritualistic way.

The emotion-charged etiquette of the Japanese was not limited to behavior in social situations; it permeated every aspect of their culture. Over the early centuries they developed precise ways of doing virtually everything in their daily existence, to the point that these ways were no longer regarded as arbitrary forms of etiquette. They became an integral part of their identity as Japanese.

The introduction of individualism, democracy and other cultural concepts from the West, which began wholesale in 1945 with the U.S. occupation of the country, has eroded the traditional etiquette of the Japanese, especially among the young. But it was so deeply embedded in the cultural and psyche of the people that much of it has survived and it is still characteristic of the majority of the Japanese in their daily behavior.

One of the characteristics of traditional Japanese etiquette that is still visible in Japan today is the smooth and harmonious way society continues to function as a whole, despite what amounts to a huge population in a very small land area.

This etiquette is conspicuously visible in the homes, in stores, on the streets, in offices, in factories, and elsewhere.

Conforming to a high standard of etiquette may be intellectually driven to some degree, but it is primarily an emotional response to others, requiring that one sup-press his or her ego and built-in selfishness on behalf of others.

The right-brain orientation of the Japanese can therefore be credited with a style and level of etiquette that has distinguished them since ancient times, and has contributed enormously to the ambiance and efficiency of Japanese culture.

Unfortunately, Japan's upcoming generations are no longer being programmed in the traditional behavioral forms, either at home or in school. They pick up on some of the forms from the older generations by osmosis, but most young people today behave very much like Westerners when they are not in formal situations.

Generally, the first formal instructions the younger generations get now is when they go to work in the adult world in companies that retain much if not all of the traditional etiquette in their corporate culture.

For the most part, the growing incidence of disharmony and violence in Japanese society can be traced directly to these changes in the etiquette system.

*

Policies Instead of Principles

In earlier times Japanese society was primarily based
on policies rather than principles—a system created
and enforced by the Shogunate governments
as a political ploy to maintain their power—and ,
further enhanced by the code of the samurai, which
often gave precedence to form and style
over human rights.

*

[8]

Policies vs. Principles

The right-brain orientation of the Japanese combined with Buddhist, Confucian and Shinto influences, resulted in Japan's culture becoming primarily human-centered rather than principle-centered.

This meant that many decisions in Japan that left-brain thinkers would make on the bases of objective principles were commonly made on the basis of human interests prevailing at that particular time and place.

The various influences on the Japanese process of thinking were so powerful that their lives were generally controlled by policies rather than principles. In fact, as late as the last decades of the 20th century, sociologists and others often complained, "We Japanese don't have principles; we have policies!"

In other words, the traditional, fundamental morality of the Japanese was circumstantial, or conditional, and was based on what the ruling power said it was. The day-to-day security and survival of the people depended upon them obeying the morality prescribed by those in power.

WHY THE JAPANESE ARE A SUPERIOR PEOPLE!

Until the introduction of democracy into Japan in 1945-46, behavior based on circumstances and policies rather than principles served Japan efficiently, if not well. In contests and other conflicts, those who do not have principles generally have an advantage.

There is now enormous economic, political and social pressure on Japan to conduct all of its affairs on the basis of well-established universal principles. And little by little, progress is being made. But a complete conversion to principle-based systems will take time. Such a fundamental change in a culture as powerful and as deeply entrenched as that of Japan is a generational thing.

Individually, most Japanese are as principled as any of their foreign counterparts may be, but generally speaking they must conform to the morality and policies of the systems they are in.

Still, it is not advisable for left-brained, principled-based, people to compromise their principles when dealing with the Japanese. The Japanese want to change the systems that control them, and often the only way they can do that is when outside pressure builds up to the point that a system change becomes the only acceptable thing to do.

Even in this area, one can find an advantage that the Japanese have when it comes to their view and use of policies. As a whole, the Japanese accept new policies that make sense quickly and completely, making it possible to implement new approaches virtually overnight—something that often does not happen in logic-oriented societies.

[9]

Aestheticism vs. Practicality

The traditional mindset of the Japanese was steeped in aestheticism as a result of the tenants of Shinto, their indigenous religion, because it was based on the worship of "nature spirits"—in particular, mountains, ancient rocks, gnarled trees, flowers and other natural phenomenon.

As the abode of spirits that controlled their survival and the quality of their lives, the Japanese treated flowers, milled lumber and building pillars, mountain peaks, scenic gorges and other manifestations of nature with ritual reverence, and became especially sensitive and respectful toward their natural beauty.

This cultural-induced sensitivity to and respect for the beauty of nature led the Japanese to strive to re-create the beauty of nature in their arts and crafts. This striving to recreate nature, combined with the master-apprentice approach to transmitting manual skills from one generation to the next, resulted in the quality of their crafts rising to the level of fine arts, reinforcing the role and importance of aesthetics in their lives.

WHY THE JAPANESE ARE A SUPERIOR PEOPLE!

But the Japanese did not stop there. Virtually all Japanese wrote poetry celebrating the beauty of nature. Skill in composing poetry was regarded as a measure of one's cultural achievements and morality. Outstanding poets won honor and lasting fame.

The Japanese went further in appreciating beauty and in exercising their aesthetic capabilities. They created a number of customs and rituals that were specifically designed for communing with the beauty and spirits of nature.

These rituals included the famous tea ceremony, flower-viewing, moon-viewing, and snow-viewing. These rituals were not just casual practices that one did now and then for relaxation. They were an important part of the cultural activities of the population.

The tea ceremony in particular, which was designed to demonstrate one's "cultural morality" and to soothe the spirit and purify the soul, became an essential part of the Japanese way of expressing their Japaneseness.

From the early 1600s until the beginning of modern times, Japan's famous samurai class spent as much time and as much energy developing their aesthetic prowess as they did honing their skill in the fighting arts.

The warrior who could not compose a poem, even under the most extreme conditions such as his imminent death, or conduct a tea ceremony with masterful grace, was considered uncultured and incomplete.

With the appearance of an affluent middle class of business people from the mid-1600s on, merchants vied with fief lords, and the members of the Shogun's court in Yedo, and the imperial court in Kyoto in staging tea ceremonies—the largest of which had as many as one thousand guests.

The unique tea ceremony and flower-viewing have survived into modern times, and continue to play a significant role in Japanese life. Both have many schools and large followings. Each spring virtually everyone in the country from teenagers to the most elderly participate in parties to celebrate the beauty of cherry blossoms.

While the aesthetic sense of the Japanese has given them a built-in advantage in business—from the design of products to packaging, displays and advertising—the emotional content of aestheticism, which is a right-brain thing, often becomes a negative factor in their conduct of business, diplomatic and political affairs.

On one occasion that I recall vividly, I experienced what then was a surprising example of the hold that aestheticism has on the Japanese mind. I was interviewing a company about a new product it had just released, but was unable to get the details needed for a story. The spokesperson kept asking me to comment on the "warm feelings" imparted by pebbles in a lobby fountain.

The aesthetic side of the Japanese character incorporates a deep-seated sense of harmony in all things, particularly in interpersonal relationships. This complicates their interacting with each other, and can be especially disadvantageous in their dealings with Westerners and other people who are not as emotion-bound and, in fact, try to separate personal feelings from their professional dealings.

Americans in particular are culturally conditioned to "grow up" and conduct their affairs in an objective, non-emotional manner—a factor that runs counter to the traditional Japanese way.

Since the Japanese must do business with the left-brain world, they are typically forced to suppress their right-brain impulses, and often to downplay or forget altogether their right-brain skills. The fact that they have been able create an economic superpower is testimony to their perseverance and ability to use both sides of their brain when pride, honor and ambition are at stake.

I suggest that the left-brain world would be much better off if it would consciously and deliberately adopt practices and customs that would help develop the right side of the brain.

[10]

Conformism Vs. Entrepreneurship

Until late 1945-46 when democratic principles were introduced into Japan by the United States, the Japanese were constrained by both custom and law from behaving as individuals. For more than two thousand years they had been physically programmed and mentally conditioned to conform to a precise etiquette and to an equally precise set of rules that controlled what they did and how they did it, including such mundane things as sweeping and mopping floors.

Throughout Japan's early history entrepreneurship—as exhibited in the West from the beginning of the Industrial Revolution—was suppressed. Until the end of Shogunate government in 1868, innovation, invention and even such practical things as building bridges across rivers was virtually banned

The ruling Shogunate government proclamation that nothing new should be invented was aimed at maintaining the political and social status quo. The injunction against building bridges was a political measure to help prevent any of the 200-plus fief warlords from attacking the Shogunate headquarters in Yedo (Tokyo).

Throughout the history of the country, the right-brain orientation of the Japanese, with all of its emotional and spiritual emphasis, was generally given precedence over other considerations. Conformism, including the most routine forms of personal behavior, became the overwhelming rule in Japanese society.

Japanese who did not conform to the prescribed attitudes and behavior were in danger of losing their place in society, and in extreme cases their identity as Japanese. Behaving in a non-Japanese manner was not only regarded as disruptive, it was considered immoral.

Until the latter decades of the 20th century one of the elements of Japanese culture that was praised the highest was the virtually complete homogenization of the Japanese mind-set and behavior.

The Japanese looked upon their homogeneity with enormous pride, and commonly pointed to it as one of their most important cultural traits, as well as a major economic and political advantage because it contributed significantly to wholehearted cooperation and mutual effort throughout society.

This, of course, was a very valid viewpoint until about 1970, by which time Japan was heavily involved in international trade and foreign affairs, popular American culture had begun to have a fundamental influence on the attitudes and behavior of the young, and millions of people had traveled abroad—all factors that had begun to build a desire for more individuality, more flexibility, and more non-Japanese spice in their lives.

During this decade, teenagers especially began to dress, talk and behave in ways that were absolutely unthinkable to their parents—to the point that sociologists began referring to them as *shinjinrui* (sheen-jeen-rooey), or "new breed of people."

When Japan's financial system tanked in 1990-1 and its amazing economic engine began to sputter, the cultural homogeneity and built-in imperative of conformity became major liabilities, resulting in a mental flip-flop, with leaders in virtually every field calling for more individuality in Japanese behavior, including more entrepreneurship.

Drastic and sometimes heroic steps were taken by many companies to change their corporate cultures to accommodate entrepreneurial behavior. But the older the company the more likely these changes could not occur within their existing frameworks, so their only choice was to establish small wholly-owned subsidiaries, staff them with young people, and make them virtually autonomous from the parent companies.

However, the deep-seated power of the traditional culture combined with the ongoing influence of language-based right-brain thinking has prevented the Japanese from totally changing their cultural and linguistic stripes, making the change from a conformist society to an entrepreneurial society a slow, incremental, generational process.

WHY THE JAPANESE ARE A SUPERIOR PEOPLE!

The more emphasis the Japanese put on learning foreign languages, the more adept they become at thinking outside of the Japanese box—and the more advantage they will have from being able to tap into both sides of their brain.

[11]

Femininity vs. Masculinity

One of the more remarkable facets of Japanese culture is the fact that it is fundamentally feminine—a factor that plays a primary role in the positive affect it has on people; especially Westerners whose cultures are more masculine oriented.

The feminine nature of Japanese culture can be traced to the influence of Shinto, which is essentially based on the role and importance of fertility in all life, and, on the emotional content of the Japanese mindset, which is a product of their right-brain orientation.

Over the centuries much of the overall refinement of Japan's arts, crafts and lifestyle resulted from the feminine side of the culture. This feminine character had an especially profound influence on the shape, finish and aura of the arts, crafts and wearing apparel.

Still today, the feminine aspects of Japanese culture are obvious in the behavior of the people, in their aesthetic appreciation, in their emotional approach to relationships, in their emphasis on humanism, and in their preference for harmony and order in their lives.

The emphasis on femininity is especially conspicuous in Japanese women, but it is also easily discernible in the character and behavior of Japanese men. Traditionally, Japanese women radiated femininity on a much higher scale than women in many other cultures, and this, of course, is the reason Western men have always found them so attractive.

While the feminine qualities of Japan's culture today have been watered down by Western masculine influences, they remain strong enough to be visible and to have a powerful impact on virtually every aspect of life in the country.

The femininity of Japanese women still draws Western men the way flame draws moths. The underlying feminine nature of Japanese things also acts as a magnet on Westerners, although this influence is mostly subconscious.

Interestingly, Western men are generally more comfortable in Japan than Western women—unless the women are into aesthetics, and both consciously and subconsciously respond in a positive way to the feminine side of the culture.

However, the attraction that Japanese culture has for typical Western males is primarily sexual, not aesthetic. In fact, many Western men who stay in Japan for long periods of time because of the feminine appeal of the women and the sensual attraction of the culture—which is mostly subconscious—have a kind of love/hate relationship with the country. One might say their testosterone holes them there against their will.

Overall, the influence of Japan's feminine culture is positive. It is the source of much of the cultural ambiance that makes life in the country so pleasing for most people. It also provides the Japanese with a number of assets that are advantageous in business—from the design and manufacture of products, to advertising, marketing and product displays in retail shops.

On the negative side, the dominant feminine nature of Japanese culture makes it difficult for the Japanese to deal with left-brain oriented cultures because they are more masculine, more direct, more "hard fact" oriented.

The influence of the more masculine cultures of the West—especially that of the United States—is gradually overlaying some of the aspects of the feminine side of Japanese culture, but it is not likely to be eroded away any time soon.

In addition to being constantly renewed by the language, feminism is so deeply embedded in the psyche of the people that even without the influence of the language it would no doubt persist for many generations. And it should be recognized, celebrated, and promoted for all of the benefits that it provides.

Just as the feminine nature of Japanese culture is an asset, the masculine nature of other cultures is a major disadvantage; what one might call a cultural failure, at least as far as evolution is concerned. The male attributes that were useful before the advent of civilization are no longer needed, and yet the primitive masculine impulse to destroy and kill is still present in the male mind.

The answer to improving Japan's relationships with the rest of the world is not for the Japanese to wean themselves away from their feminine side, but for left-brain dominant people to add a feminine element to their cultures through education and practice in using the right side of their brains.

[12]
Humanism vs. Scientism

Industrialization was introduced into Japan in 1870 by a new crop of Japanese leaders who had defeated the feudal shogunate government and were determined to catch up with the West in terms of industry and military power in order to avoid being colonized—and to demonstrate aspects of their culture that they considered superior to Western ways.

Up to that time, the primary thrust of Japan's shogunate government had been to maintain the status quo, politically, socially and economically—to prevent changes of any kind that would undermine its control of the country.

For the preceding 230-plus years this prevention took the form of isolating Japan from the rest of the world. In addition to this drastic political action, the Japanese had been culturally conditioned for close to a thousand years to revere the past; to look backward instead of forward.

These political and cultural factors emphasized humanism and downplayed or ignored altogether research and the natural sciences. Thus there had been almost no invention and no innovation in Japan since the ascendancy of the warrior class as the rulers of Japan in 1192.

The miniscule amount of modern science and technology that existed in Japan before the 1850s had entered the country through a tiny crack that was left open to Dutch traders on a manmade islet in Nagasaki Bay that was connected to the mainland by a narrow causeway blocked off by a huge gate and guarded 24-hours a day by samurai warriors—a remarkable situation that began in1641 and lasted until 1868.

Disinterest in scientific research was built into Japanese culture by the dominance of the right side of their brains, and was, in fact, blocked by the shogunate government, which saw it as a major danger to its supremacy.

One of the more remarkable episodes in Japanese history was a decision by the shogunate government in the 1600s to ban the use of guns [originally introduced into the country by Portuguese traders in 1543], as being "un-Japanese" and disruptive to the Japanese way of life.

Thus it came about that the humanism in Japanese culture took precedence over scientism until 1870, when the leaders of the new government set Japan on the left-brain path of industrialization and a Western-type economy.

As with so many other legacies of the traditional culture, humanism did not disappear from the scene when industrialization began. The new Western type business that were set up by the thousands were organized and managed according to right-brain humanistic precepts that had been a part of Japan's culture since day one.

Furthermore, the humanistic traditions of the Japanese did prevent them from embracing scientism as soon as they were politically free to do so. From 1870, thousands of well-educated and ambitious Japanese began innovating and inventing with extraordinary enthusiasm and diligence.

This enthusiasm and diligence became even more pronounced following the end of World War II in 1945, and soon developed into an obsession that has continued to grow.

Despite this amazing switch to left-brain research, the Japanese did not give up their humanistic approach to management. As late as the 1980s, they took great pride in contrasting their humanistic approach to business with the "anti-human" policies and practices of American and other Western companies.

It was not until the "Big Bang" in the early 1990s when Japan's "bubble economy" suddenly began to lose power that the fabled humanism of the Japanese began to take a backseat to the left-brain management practices that included firing employees, closing factories and dispensing with the seniority-based system of wages. One of the challenges the Japanese face now is not to lose all of their commitment to humanism in order to compete with other countries.

In the meantime, American, European and other Western companies have been under increasing pressure to humanize their management practices since the

1980s and 90s, and many have done so successfully—a somewhat ironic switch from their left-brain way of doing things.

Japanese style humanism will no doubt assume more and more importance in all areas of life everywhere, not only in business management but in all fields of endeavor, especially in science, which now more often than not first serves the interest of military power before it gets down to the interest of the people.

*

Cultural Programming in Groupism

The *shudan ishiki* [shuu-dahn eesh-kee] or "group consciousness" of the Japanese is deeply rooted in the culture, and derives from the homogenizing effects of living for centuries within the confines of a carefully programmed social system that controlled thoughts as well as actions.

*

[13]

Groupism vs. Individualism

From the dawn of their history, the Japanese have been encouraged, directed and generally forced to think and behave as groups rather than individuals. In fact, during most of Japan's history individualistic behavior was not only considered immoral, in many instances it was against the law and could have fatal consequences.

One of the best-known Japanese proverbs notes that the person who stands out like a nail gets hammered down. Over the centuries this cultural imperative was so powerful that it was not until the 1990s, when the Japanese economy was shaken by a financial meltdown, that one began to hear calls for individualism, for entrepreneurship, and for "non-Japanese" thinking to get the economy back on an upward path.

During Japan's remarkable rise to economic superpowdom between 1945 and 1970 the social and corporate sanctions against individualistic behavior were very real and very harsh. People who were unusually intelligent or experienced and talented had to be extraordinarily careful not to bring the wrath of their co-workers down on them, or to be totally ignored or transferred to some meaningless job by their employers.

From 1960 until about 1980 thousands of individuals who had studied abroad to increase their technical skills and/or improve on their foreign language abilities—many of them actually sent abroad by their own companies—were treated as pariahs when they returned to Japan. Other thousands left Japan to take up research in other countries because their independent thinking and individualistic behavior was not tolerated by whatever company or organization they belonged to.

The fact that some of these individuals went on to achieve extraordinary success in their research [including winning Nobel Prizes] created a storm of criticism about the traditional social, economic and political sanctions against independent thinking and individualistic behavior.

These criticisms, combined with continuing concerns about Japan's economic future, resulted in weakening the anti-individualism mindset that had been drummed into the Japanese since ancient times, but it is still a major factor in every facet of Japanese life today and is not likely to disappear altogether in the foreseeable future.

The natural native propensity of the Japanese to think and act as groups was significantly influenced by their right-brain orientation, which emphasizes human feelings and harmony in all relationships, and requires putting the group before the individual.

WHY THE JAPANESE ARE A SUPERIOR PEOPLE!

All of the religious and philosophical teachings that played a role in the creation of Japan's traditional culture, beginning with Shinto, and then including Buddhism and Confucianism, were also oriented toward group behavior and group responsibility.

Obviously, there is extraordinary merit in both individualism and groupism, either in combination or with each having its own time and place. A significant degree of Japan's extraordinary economic success between 1945 and 1990 was based on the ability of the people to work in groups in which harmony was virtually absolute.

But that was when Japan was still in a kind of time warp, operating under the same mindset that was forged during its long, mostly isolated, feudal period (1192-1868). The introduction of international competition domestically as well as internationally, and the changes that occurred worldwide began to erode the benefits that had long accrued to the exclusively group approach.

While individualistic Americans are now striving to develop a more cooperative group-oriented culture, the Japanese are faced with the challenge of learning how to deal with and taken advantage of the power of individualism that is inherent in human nature.

But again, this drive for individualism should not get so far out of hand that it replaces the power of working together and the cohesiveness that such cooperation brings to society.

[14]

Harmony vs. Reality

The harmony that was characteristic of Japanese society for most of the history of the country made it necessary to suppress many of the characteristics that are inherent in all human beings, from egoism and personal interest to the fact that people are born with different temperaments, and regardless of the homogeneity of the environment they grow up in they typically end up with different personalities.

The harmony that existed in pre-modern Japan was based in part on the cultural indoctrination they got from Shinto, Buddhism and Confucianism. But it was obedience to the laws of the shogunate government that made this harmony the foundation of society. These laws, based on the samurai code of ethics that had been institutionalized and ritualized over the centuries, covered virtually every facet of behavior, and were strictly enforced. More often than not, the fate of lawbreakers was death—often on the spot.

Generally speaking, harmony in pre-modern Japan took precedence over virtually all other considerations, which often made it necessary to suppress facts, the truth and especially human feelings. Duty and obligations came first, no matter what the personal consequences.

This cultural phenomenon gave birth to the custom of concealing the truth by speaking in ambiguous terms and by using the ingenious artifice described as *tatemae* (tah-tay-my) and *honne* (hone-nay), noted earlier.*

Tatemae refers to a verbal façade that one presents as a front, in order to avoid exposing one's *honne*, or real intentions, at the beginning of a dialogue or negotiation. The idea being that the dialogue will continue until both sides gradually reveal their true positions, without either side losing or gaining an advantage over the other, while maintaining carefully controlled harmony—a custom that is still characteristic of Japanese behavior today.

Not being aware of this cultural trait in Japanese behavior, the first Westerners in Japan in the 16th century often described them as habitual liars, unable to tell the truth. In fact, it was not until the last half of the 20th century that knowledge of this cultural trait became generally known to outsiders.

---

*I introduced the *tatemae* and *honne* cultural factor to Western businessmen in my book, *Japanese Etiquette & Ethics in Business*, first published in 1959 and still in print at McGraw-Hill.

In present-day Japan, harmony still takes precedence over reality, but it is weaker than before and is very slowly giving away to the give-and-take kind of inter-action that is favored by Americans. However, it is still considered a serious breach of etiquette to take a blunt, hard approach to any subject at the onset of any conversation.

As in virtually all other areas of typical Japanese behavior the role and importance of harmony was, and still is, an outgrowth of the right-brained emotional content in the Japanese mind-set. The average Japanese simply cannot avoid reacting to things emotionally, and reading a great deal more into situations than they often require or deserve.

There are exceptions, of course, among Japanese who have had substantial experience in interacting with Westerners, especially if they are able to communicate in English or any other left-brain language. But these exceptions may be little more than skin deep, and still not reflect reality.

Since the early 1990s a growing number of Japanese who have become bilingual and at least partially bicultural have been haranguing their fellow countrymen to break out of this linguistic-based mold in other to communicate more clearly and completely with others.

The Japanese are acutely aware of this factor in their relationships with others, but it is a cultural mold that is very difficult to break, and will no doubt continue to be characteristic of their behavior for some time.

The challenge for the Japanese is to develop the diplomatic skills that will make it possible for them to dispense with *tatemae* altogether, and communicate only their *honne*.

*

Sanctions Enforce Harmony

Social harmony, based on following prescribed etiquette in daily behavior [under the threat of being ostracized], remains the guiding principle in all Japanese relationships; personal, business and political.

*

[15]
Passivity vs. Aggression

Another of the dichotomies in the Japanese character that is greatly influenced by their right-brain orientation has to do with passivity and aggression. For centuries Japanese who were not members of the ruling samurai class were conditioned by their culture and compelled by their system of government to behave in an extraordinarily passive manner.

This passivity was based on precise forms of behavior toward everyone, but especially toward superiors and those with any kind of official authority. The sanctions enforcing this passivity were powerful and generally unforgiving. Two of the measures that were constantly over the heads of the common people like a sword were immediate death at the hands of a samurai warrior, and being ostracized by their group.

This conditioning in passivity during the long reign of the shoguns (1192-1868) was so comprehensive that it became second nature to the common people—and gave early visitors to Japan the impression that ordinary Japanese were among the most peaceful and polite people on the planet.

And generally speaking this was in fact true. By the same token, however, the Japanese were so susceptible to being controlled and molded by those in authority that they could be turned from their peaceful ways to acts of extreme violence in a very short period of time, as was starkly demonstrated by their wartime activities in the first half of the 20th century.

Still today, under normal circumstances, the Japanese are far more passive-minded than most Westerners, and they continue to accept regimentation more readily than others.

Individual aggression, especially in public, is still rare in Japan, although this too is increasing as the power of the traditional culture weakens. When aggressive behavior does occur it can be explosive because once the cultural restraints on such behavior are removed by some official edict, or thrown off in a personal action, the results can be extreme.

Emotional outbursts that lead to violence have also become more common in Japan, including in the Diet. These actions are caused by the fact that the Japanese have had little experience in the kind of hard-ball but civilized debating that takes place in government halls in the U.S., England and Europe.

Such give-and-take behavior is precisely the kind of exchanges that was taboo in traditional Japan, because it contradicted the imperative of harmony.

Because harmony traditionally took priority over the expression of emotion in Japan, the Japanese lived in a pressure cooker for generations; very calm on the surface but often seething with unfulfilled needs and unresolved anger.

The lid of this cultural pressure cooker was first unbolted in 1945 by the abolition of the feudalist family system and the removal of social, political and economic sanctions on independent thinking and behaving.

This gift of freedom did not immediately change the attitudes or behavior of most adult Japanese, especially the men. The conditioning they had been subjected to throughout their lives was too strong. Young women were the first to take advantage of this new freedom—since women are always more flexible and more practical than men [as a survival method].

The first generation of Japanese to escape much of the cultural conditioning that was responsible for the passive mind-set of their parents and ancestors were those born after 1960, and it was this generation that began to weaken the cultural molds of the past.

And yet again, the power of the traditional culture and the language is such that most Japanese still today live partially or totally within the cultural molds of the past. The lid is still on the cooker, and most Japanese must conform, emotionally and intellectually, to the dictates of their environment.

The challenge today is for the Japanese to try to achieve a better balance between the emotional side of their character and the objective, logical input from the left side of their brains.

*

Losing the Samurai Spirit

Japan's samurai-honed culture imbued the Japanese with a powerful spirit that was religious in nature [meaning it was based on a philosophy and ideology founded on faith, not facts], and it was this indomitable spirit that motivated and sustained the Japanese in all of their efforts in work as well as war—even in their sports.
It was this spirit that drove the Japanese to rebuild their country and their self-respect after the end of World War II. But this generation has mostly gone and the cultural programming that created and kept the spirit alive has diminished to the point that it is no longer paramount in the lives of the
post-war generations.
This is a serious threat to the superiority of the Japanese, and present-day attempts to rekindle the Japanese spirit are too little and may be too late.

*

WHY THE JAPANESE ARE A SUPERIOR PEOPLE!

[16]

Spirit vs. Reality

Another of the primary elements of the Japanese character that is heavily influenced by their right-brain orientation and its reservoir of emotions is their spirit—that is their will, their motivation; the combined brain power that drives them.

Very early in their history the Japanese became endowed with a spirit that they regarded as one of their most distinguishing and valuable characteristics. This spirit was called *Yamato damashii* (Yah-mah-toh dah-mah-she-ee), or "Japanese spirit," and was seen as the primary essence of the Japanese character and the foundation of their national identity.

The phrase first came into use over a thousand years ago to distinguish between native ideas, and patterns of thought imported from China. [Yamato was the original name the Japanese gave to their country, apparently taken from the name of the clan that founded the Imperial line.]

Later, the phrase was used in literary works and in military treatises to describe spiritual qualities that were supposedly unique to the Japanese, and included such attributes as devotion to country, sincerity, courage, strength of mind and the ability to endure pain and adversity.

Following the fall of the shogunate form of government in 1868 the *Yamato damashii* concept was made the foundation of the training and indoctrination of the country's new Western style military forces. It was also made the cornerstone of the public school system.

This was the spirit that the new government invoked when it began a crash program to catch up with the West industrially and militarily. It was also the spirit that was called upon to inspire Japan's military forces during World War II, especially after it became obvious that the country was going to be defeated for the first time in its history.

Because they were totally programmed in the idea that spirit would bring them victory over a much larger and more powerful adversary, the Japanese fought with incredible tenacity and courage, and having lost the war, turned this same spirit into rebuilding Japan and transforming their country into the world's second largest economy.

The spirit of the Japanese is still strong and still provides them with the will and energy that is reflected not only in their economic prowess, but also in the efficiency with which they operate their economy. It is the source of their drive for quality in everything they do.

[17]

Quality vs. Profit

One of the most extraordinary differences in the traditional culture of Japan and the post-Industrial cultures of the United States and Europe was that in Japan profit-making was regarded as immoral, while in these Western countries making a profit was the primary goal of all privately owned enterprises.

In the context of Japan's traditional culture, profit making was counter to the teachings of Buddhism and to the Japanese concept of humanism. In the Japanese view, the fundamental purpose of an enterprise was to provide an essential service to society.

During the last centuries of shogunate Japan (1603-1868) there were even laws controlling profit-making, and there were occasions when the government confiscated companies that were conspicuously profitable.

Instead of being driven by the profit motive, the Japanese were driven by a compulsion to achieve the highest possible quality in everything they made. This compulsion was energized by the master-apprentice approach to all work, which generally was not constrained by short time frames. Apprenticeships commonly lasted for ten to fifteen years and could last for thirty years or even longer. Artists and craftsmen often refused commissions that had deadlines.

This system gave birth to the attitude that it was the primary duty of every artist and craftsman to continuously try to achieve perfection throughout their lifetimes. Over the centuries this raised the level of quality in many fields to that of fine arts. Even the most mundane kitchen utensils became works of art.

This is not to say that commercialism and profit making did not exist in pre-modern Japan. During the long and peaceful period of the last shogunate, the government could not exercise sufficient control over merchants to prevent them from making and disguising profits, and over the 200-plus years of that era many of them became wealthy.

In 1870 the new government of Japan began a top-down program of industrializing the country, providing the financing for all of the basic industries and then turning them over to favored family groups like Mitsui, Mitsubishi, Sumitomo, Yasuda, Asano, Nissan, and half a dozen others that came to be known as *zaibatsu* (zigh-bot-sue), or "financial cliques," all of which were to become immensely rich and powerful.

In other words, the profit motive was officially introduced into Japan in the early 1870s by the new government because it was motivated by an incredibly powerful compulsion to catch up with the Western countries.

But the concept that the primary role of enterprises was to serve the public was so deeply embedded in the psyche of the Japanese that it did not disappear altogether. Many of the new entrepreneurs who founded companies during the first decades of the 1900s were still primarily motivated by traditional beliefs, and mixed their commercialism with the social obligations they felt toward their employees, communities and the country at large.

Two of the most outstanding figures who followed this pattern were Sazo Idemitsu, who established the forerunner of Idemitsu Oil Company in 1911, and Konosuke Matsushita who founded what was to become the Matsushita Electric Industrial Company in 1918 and Panasonic in 2008.

Both Idemitsu and Matsushita preached and practiced the policy of living humble lives and managing their companies to provide the best possible products to society at an affordable price. Even though they had to make a profit, profits came after product quality and service to the public. Their philosophy was that if they made the best products that could be made and served the public with absolute sincerity and diligence, the public would buy from them and they would make a profit.

It is still accurate to say that among the vast majority of Japanese companies, quality and service are regarded as important as profits. And while the origin of this philosophy can no doubt be traced to the influence of Shinto and Buddhism, the overall humanistic values of the Japanese grew out of the right-brain influence on their mindset.

Japanese companies must now compete on price with foreign firms that generally adjust their quality standards to squeeze as much profit as possible out of their products. This is making it increasingly difficult for the Japanese to maintain their standards.

So far the Japanese have managed to compete on the basis of both quality and price by utilizing superior manufacturing and testing procedures that virtually eliminate defective products. But there may be a limit to how long they can depend upon this approach, as a growing number of American and other firms have adopted—and sometimes improved on—the Japanese techniques of manufacturing without defects.

If Japanese companies can hang onto the philosophy that quality and service are on the same plane as profit, they will be among those that deserve to survive into the future.*

---

*Virtually all foreign businesspeople worldwide are now familiar with the Japanese term *kaizen* (kigh-zen), meaning "continuous improvement" [which I introduced to the Western world in the early 1960s]. Many, however, are not aware that Japan's arts and crafts had reached the level of fine arts as much as a thousand years ago, and once Japanese manufacturers were able to get out from under the control of foreign importers in the late 1950s and early 1960s, the quality of their products shot skyward. The Japanese referred to their high quality standards as *atarimae no hinshitsu* (ah-tah-ree-my no heen-sheet-sue), or "ordinary-natural-expected quality." In the following decades, many manufacturers raised this level of quality to what they referred to as *haisensu* (high-sense) quality.

[18]

Diligence vs. Getting By

One of the traditional cultural elements in the character of the Japanese was a sense of *kinben* [keen-bane] or diligence that virtually knew no bounds. This element derived from an amalgamation of Shinto and Zen Buddhism that was honed to a sharp edge by the samurai warrior class that ruled Japan from 1192 until 1868, and whose standard was perfection in all things.

Diligence, on the highest possible level, was not only expected by the samurai class, it was required, and broadly speaking there were serious consequences for those who failed to live up to their *kinben* standards—standards that gradually became an integral part of the common culture.

Not being totally diligent in one's efforts—regardless of the outcome—was considered shameful and un-Japanese, and that was something the Japanese could not stand. They were exceedingly sensitive to shame and any sign of disrespect, and were thus motivated to extend themselves in whatever they did.

In this social environment unstinting effort was the key to approval and respect, and was praised and honored.

Here again, this mindset primarily derived from the emotional content of the Japanese character. Rather than taking an objective, rational approach to quitting when things got hard, and when they appeared to be impossible, the Japanese were prompted by their feelings to redouble their efforts.

This trait has, of course, long been visible in Japanese behavior; going back to the days of the samurai, to their military endeavors in more recent times, and finally in their extraordinary feat of not only rebuilding Japan after World War II, but transforming the country into an economic superpower in just two and a half decades.

This cultural importance of diligence is still one of the primary elements in the attributes of most present-day Japanese, and still today gives Japanese companies an advantage over foreign companies. There are exceptions on the foreign side, or course, but they are exceptions not the rule, and this makes a fundamental difference in the productivity and competitive power of individual companies.

However, by the late 1990s the famous diligence of Japanese workers had begun to noticeably erode and that of American and other workers had continued to improve—again primarily because of real and perceived competition from Japan.

By the end of the 20th century much of the indoctrination of diligence by Japanese parents and schools had diminished significantly, resulting in the first generation in which there were large numbers of individuals who were less motivated and less diligent than those who came before them.

While the influence of the Japanese language on this new generation remains strong, the emotional content of their character is no longer channeled into behavior marked by diligence, and the number of Japanese who are far less diligent than older generations is growing exponentially.

If this trend continues—and it surely will—it will have a profoundly negative influence on the future of Japan.

As for the "just enough to get by" trend that began to afflict American workers in the 1950s, the downward movement appears to have slowed dramatically, and from around 1975 began inching upward—again, primarily because of competition from Japan, which at that time seemed destined to economically colonize the world.

If Japan is to retain its position as an economic superpower it must once again make the concept and practice of diligence a primary part of the Japanese character. If the U.S. is to regain and maintain its ability to compete with the new superpowers of Asia the importance of diligence will have to be given far more attention than what it gets today.

WHY THE JAPANESE ARE A SUPERIOR PEOPLE!

*

Risk-Taking in U.S.
vs.
Risk-Taking in Japan

One of the primary factors in the rise of the United States to political and economic prominence was the willingness of Americans to take risks in virtually every aspect of their lives—something that came about because the first Americans broke their bonds with the stifling cultures of Europe, and had a sparsely settled continent to take and make their own
virtually free of charge.
The vast majority of ordinary Japanese, on the other hand, from the beginning of their history until the 1950s, were not free to innovate or take financial and economic risks.
Still today most risk-taking in Japan is carefully controlled and is spread out among several entities as opposed to personal ventures by individuals.

*

[19]

Risk-Aversion vs. Risk-Taking

With the exception of ill-founded military ventures that ended in 1945, the Japanese have traditionally been adverse to risk-taking, not only on a national scale but down to the attitudes and behavior of individuals.

In this case, the risk-aversion mindset of the Japanese did not derive primarily from their right-brain orientation—which one might assume would have made them more likely to take risks because they were drive more by emotion and an exaggerated spirit than by rational thinking.

In fact, it was this emotion-charged spirit that led Japanese leaders to engage in military adventures that ended in Japan's defeat in World War II, and brought home to the Japanese the folly of spirit-driven risk taking.

The Japanese have traditionally had an aversion to risk-taking because of cultural factors that had very little to do the dominance of the right side of their brains—although this factor made their aversion to risking-taking stronger.

Their aversion to risk-taking developed in ancient times because their social and political systems made it both immoral and dangerous. In harmony-conscious Japan, anything that might result in disharmony was taboo. Risk-taking on any level can be disruptive when it fails, so it was bad.

As time passed, this aversion to risk-taking permeated the mindset of the people, and was further buttressed by the prevailing philosophy of group-orientation and decision-making by consensus—both of which were designed to reduce the danger of risk-taking by making such actions difficult to carry out and avoiding personal responsibility when something did go wrong.

The influence of these cultural factors is still very obvious in present-day Japan. Risk-taking is still looked upon as immoral to some degree, and as a last resort when there is absolutely no other choice.

This factor is a primary element in the tendency for Japanese companies to form consortiums and groups when undertaking ventures that involve some risk, and to deal only with Japanese companies when there is a choice.

However, by the beginning of the 21st century the aversion to risk that had been built into Japan's culture had become a major handicap, not only internationally but domestically as well. Consultants, educators and others had begun to preach that the Japanese had to discard the old way of thinking and behaving, and begin taking risks.

But the older and larger the Japanese company, the more difficult it is for it to change its ways. The older individual managers and executives, the more likely they are to fear and shy away from risk-taking. But they are acutely aware of the need for a new mindset.

Many of these companies have established small, wholly-owed subsidiaries, staffed them with young employees, and given them the authority to take risks because there is simply no other way for them to gain the advantage of carefully planned gambling on a new product or service.

Despite substantial progress in suppressing the age-old cultural taboos against risk-taking and the right-brain fears of failure, the combination of these two factors continue to influence the Japanese and must be dealt with in dealing with them.

On the plus side, the Japanese are now much more willing to accept foreigner investors and partners, and to follow through on their famous *kyosei* (k'yoh-say-ee) concept of global economic integration.

*

Reverting to Traditional Management

In the 1950s several large Japanese companies replaced their traditional Japanese style of management with the American management style. All of the companies that made this big switch went broke, and most of them disappeared.
Japan's astounding economic growth from the mid-1950s to the 1970s was propelled by Japanese style management.
But growing competition from foreign firms, both domestically and internationally, began to erode the efficiency of the Japanese way of running their companies, and little by little they began integrating Western business practices into their management systems.
Interestingly, by 2008 more powerful competition from abroad had begun to take the bloom off of Western management. Now, there is a slow but growing move to resurrect some of the traditional Japanese ways of management.

*

[20]

Sincerity vs. Insincerity

The Japanese have traditionally regarded themselves as among the most sincere people on the planet—a belief that grew out of their commitment to harmony, which incorporated a cooperative attitude, humility, honesty, veracity, respect and goodwill—all Japanese style, of course.

While this commitment to harmony was reinforced by their right-brain qualities of spirituality, attunement with nature and humanistic feelings, the core of their sincerity evolved out of the obligations they owed to the social and political systems under which they lived, particularly following the beginning of rule by the samurai class in 1192.

The warrior-administered government simply imposed a system of laws on the people that were designed to ensure harmony, and then enforced the laws with stern measures that guaranteed they would be obeyed.

Over the centuries, the Japanese were thus mentally and physically programmed to behave in a precise manner that came to be equated with sincerity in all things—a type of behavior that would ensure harmony in all human relationships.

In essence, this meant that the Japanese would not do anything that would result in friction or disharmony, which typically meant suppressing their emotions, doing things they did not want to do, and being tolerant of the behavior of others in the expectation of receiving similar treatment in the future.

In short, the Japanese definition of sincerity is doing whatever is necessary to create and sustain harmony in all relationships. Insincerity is any attitude or behavior that disrupts the harmony of the group or the enterprise.

In the past, there was also a tendency for the Japanese to regard the Western custom of resorting to hard facts and logic in decision-making as a form of insincerity, because such behavior frequently ignored human feelings and individual needs, which in traditional Japanese values had the highest priority.

Although weakened by shifts in cultural values, this cultural concept is still very much alive in the mindset of the Japanese, and is still discernible in their day-to-day behavior in business as well as in social relationships—a factor that foreign businesspeople find disconcerting if they are not aware of why it exists and how it works.

[21]

Wet vs. Dry

When the Japanese first began to encounter Westerners in the 1540s they quickly became aware that there were fundamental differences in their attitudes and behavior regarding virtually everything, from bathing (which the Japanese did daily, and the Westerners hardly every did) and food to sex—not to mention the conduct of business and personal relationships.

Many of these differences were not only visible because they involved physical behavior, they were also shocking to the Japanese, whose etiquette and lifestyle were highly organized according to precise patterns of behavior that went back centuries.

However, these differences did not have any tangible effect on the vast majority of the Japanese at that time, because they never as much as seen Westerners, much less interacted with them in any way.

It was not until the 1850s and beyond that relatively small numbers of Japanese in main cities like Yedo (Tokyo) began to occasionally see Westerners. By the late 1800s there were several thousand Westerners in Japan, but still most Japanese never saw any of them.

In fact, it was not until the fall of 1945 and the following seven years, during which there were several hundred thousand Westerners in Japan including some in the more remote areas of the country that Japanese and Westerners began to interact in large numbers, both officially and unofficially.

This interaction between hundreds of thousand of Japanese and Westerners took place on every level of society, from the top of the political heap and the business elite, down to employees in shops, bars, inns, restaurants and other facilities.

It was the unofficial interaction between Japanese women and Westerner men that was to have the fastest, the most conspicuous, and the most fundamental impact on the culture of the country. Less than a year after the arrival of Western Occupation forces in Japan, daily liaisons between the troops and young women numbered in the hundreds of thousands.

The economic contributions the free-spending GI's made to Japan's war-devastated economy amounted to millions of dollars a month. The volume of American goods diverted into the black-market was astounding. The cultural changes that were to remake Japan over the next decades began among the ranks of the young women employed by and serving the Occupation forces.

By the early 1950s popular interest magazines had begun to cover these foreign-Japanese liaisons, and to highlight the cultural the differences of the people involved. One especially astute writer began referring to the Japanese as "wet" and to Westerners as "dry,"—a phraseology that I believe originated with another writer in the 1920s.

In its Japanese context, a "wet" person is one who gives precedence to emotions and feelings—in other words a right-brained oriented Japanese. A "dry" person is one who automatically applies reason and logic to every situation he or she confronts, whether it is business or a private matter—in other words, a left-brained non-Japanese.

The 1950s writer went on to provide warnings for young Japanese women involved with foreign men. Some of his warnings were that foreign men were too objective, too unfeeling, to be suitable for Japanese women, and that foreign men would use them and then leave them.

In an ironic twist, young Japanese women today often criticize Japanese men for being too dry—uncaring and cold—while the image of foreign men has been more or less reversed, and they are now seen as wetter than their Japanese counterparts.

As soon as the American Occupation authorities allowed Westerner businessmen to enter Japan in the late 1940s they, too, began to encounter the dry-wet phenomenon, although it was not generally referred to in this terminology.

In addition to the basic communications problem resulting from the fact that the Western businesspeople invariably did not speak Japanese and it was left up to the Japanese to overcome the language barrier, both sides suffered from clashes between their wet and dry natures.

Since that long ago time, Japanese businesspeople have become dryer. Significant numbers of them can communicate in English or other Western languages, and they have had more than a generation of experience dealing with left-brain people.

For their part, most Western businesspeople dealing with the Japanese are now far more culturally sensitive and knowledgeable, thousands have spent years in Japan, and many now speak the language well.

All these things combined have taken much of the friction and pain out of Japanese-foreign business relationships. But the basic differences between wet and dry people are such that problems still arise, and it requires special effort to build and sustain harmonious relationships.

As with most of Japan's other cultural traits that evolved from their right-brain orientation, their "wet" characteristics are in tune with fundamental changes taking place in all societies—meaning that the humanistic approach to life is gradually coming into its own.

[22]

Right-Brain Views That Distinguish the Japanese

Aesthetics / *Bigaku* (Be-gah-kuu]

The Japanese view and use of aesthetics is one of their most conspicuous characteristics, distinguishing them, at least to some extent, from virtually all other people on the planet—a factor that helps to corroborate Dr. Tadano Tsunoda's theory that the Japanese are right-brain oriented.

 Aesthetics, a dominant factor in Japanese culture, is a manifestation of feelings, of emotions, which brain authorities say are processed by the right side of the brain. One might say, in fact, that the whole of Japanese culture is based on aesthetics, making the culture unique.

 There were no areas of Japan's traditional lifestyle that did not have a significant aesthetic element. Their arts, their crafts, their wearing apparel, their presentation of food, their stylized etiquette, all were infused with aesthetic elements. Even the ritual of *harakiri* (hah-rah-kee-ree), or suicide by slicing the stomach open, was performed with aesthetic style.

Obviously, people who are left-brain oriented are fully capable of recognizing and appreciating beauty, but in the majority of left-brained people aesthetics is not a primary controlling factor in their thinking and behavior, and plays only a minor role in their daily lives.

This is especially true of left-brain oriented men, with the exceptions generally being those whose female side is strong enough to influence their attitudes and behavior.

Of course, left-brained men who are homosexual are primarily motivated by feminine instincts, which accounts for their emphasis on feelings and their refined tastes.

The right-brained based aesthetic foundation of Japanese culture has proven to be one of their most valuable assets in virtually every field of endeavor, providing elements of beauty, harmony, and sophistication that are pleasing to the body, the mind and the soul.

The Japanese traditionally came by this asset naturally because it is built into the culture. But they did not stop there. They devised a variety of practices that were designed specifically to exercise and expand their aesthetic abilities.

While only a small percentage of the Japanese today actively engage in aesthetic practices on a regular basis, all continue to be influenced by the ongoing aesthetic content of the culture. And Japan as a whole continues to benefit from this remarkable aspect of the culture.

Apparel / *Fuku* [Fuu-kuu]

There are two primary factors in the Japanese view and reaction to wearing apparel. One of them is a manifestation of the influence of their right-brain orientation. The other is the fact that during the last Shogunate sysem of government (1603-1868), the clothing the Japanese were allowed to wear was prescribed by the government, and was based on their social class and occupation.

The right-brain orientation of the Japanese on their perspective of clothing is primarily feminine; that is, it is primarily based on emotions, on feelings, which results in them being exceptionally sensitive about the fabric, the color, the design and the finish of the clothing.

This special sensitivity to clothing is most obvious in the traditional kimono and *yukata* (yuu-kah-tah), in which the imperative harmony and compatibility include both the gender and the age of the individual wearer.

Government control of the apparel the Japanese were allowed to wear during the Tokugawa Shogunate era made the Japanese extraordinarily sensitive to clothing because it designated one's legal, hereditary social class. Wearing clothing that was not approved for one's class was against the law.

The laws regarding wearing apparel were so detailed that they included the precise date in the spring when the population was required to change from winter to summer clothing, and again in the fall when the whole country changed back to winter clothing [regardless of the weather on those particular dates].

By the latter decades of the 17th century, members of the merchant class who had become affluent began to circumvent this law by wearing expensive and colorful underclothing beneath their drab outer robes.

Laws controlling what the Japanese could wear disappeared in 1868 when the Tokugawa Shogunate was abolished, but some urban Japanese had been ignoring the laws with impunity for several years.

With the influx of Western technology and Western ideas from 1870 on, urban Japanese also began gradually switching over to Western style clothing. One of the factors that played a key role in this changeover was the appearance of streetcars and trains. It was difficult, and sometimes virtually impossible, for people wearing tight-fitting kimono to step up into these new forms of transportation with their dignity intact.

It was not until the years following the end of World War II in 1945 that virtually all Japanese made the switch to the more practical Western style clothing. The kimono remained the formal dress of both men and women, but it was generally worn only on special occasions, such as weddings and official ceremonies.

However, the thin, cotton *yukata* (yuu-kah-tah) robe continued to be worn around the house and as bathrobe, as well as the apparel of choice during participation in festivals and at hot spring spas—and still today continues to be a common item in the Japanese wardrobe.

Ready-made clothing in Japan today is, of course, overwhelmingly Western in style and reflects the sensibilities of Westerners, but the right-brain character of the Japanese makes them conspicuously more style and quality conscious than the typical Westerner.

Art / *Geijutsu* [Gay-jute-sue]

Most of Japan's art traditions were introduced into the country by Chinese and Korean immigrants between 300 and 700 A.D., and most were a part of the paraphernalia of Buddhism.

But over the following centuries they became Japanized as a result of a unique mindset that continues to distinguish the Japanese today.

A significant facet of this unique mindset is a product of the right-brain orientation of the Japanese—their built-in propensity to take an emotional, humanistic approach to virtually everything they do. As a result of this orientation, Japanese art has an aesthetic and philosophical quality that reflects the unique sense of the Japanese.

Traditional Japanese art generally consists of a dream-like view of nature, with the details only suggested, leaving it up to the viewer to fill in the image from his or her own view of nature. In those arts and crafts where there is more detail, the subjects are imbued with a humanistic touch that brings out the gentle spirituality of the subject. Harmony, tranquility and a sense of soulful repose are hallmarks of Japanese art.

Beauty / *Utsukushisa* [Ute-sue-kuu-shc-sah]

The Japanese are, I believe, the only people whose traditional culture included the recognition and appreciation of beauty as one of its primary elements, and who succeeded in surviving, along with the beauty-based aspects of their culture, into modern times.

It appears that the impulse that was responsible for the Japanese attachment to beauty grew out of Shinto, the indigenous religion of the Japanese, which was essentially nature worship, and which was dramatically influenced by the extraordinary beauty of the Japanese islands.

In any event, the Japanese concept of beauty grew out of nature. That which was natural was beautiful, and was to be respected and emulated. Customs and rituals to commune with the beauty of nature, and with man-made objects that emulated nature, became an integral part of the life of the people.

With nature as the standard of beauty by which all things were judged, the Japanese went on to develop vocabulary that expressed specific qualities of beauty, making it possible to describe and discuss them.

One of the key words in this vocabulary was *shibui* (she-booey), which in its aesthetic sense means simple and refined, with all extraneous parts eliminated, leaving the essence of the object revealed. Another key aesthetic term was *yugen* (yuu-gane), meaning "mystery" or "subtlety," referring to a type of beauty that lies beneath the surface of the material but is in delicate harmony with it, and registers on both the conscious and subconscious mind of the viewer. *Yugen* radiates a kind of spiritual essence.

A third term in the aesthetic vocabulary of the Japanese is *myo* (m'yoh), which by itself means strangeness or mystery, combined with skill. Japan's famed Zen master Daisetsu Suzuki said that *myo* is the expression of a quality that transcends the skill of the artist or craftsman and is a reflection of the cosmic spirit that is inherent in things.

Suzuki adds that the reason why so few Westerners are able to "see" the *myo* of art and craft objects is that their concept of beauty is based on conscious realization, with the result that their ego prevents them from seeing beyond the mechanical skill of the maker. He also says that it is the *myo* of Japanese arts and crafts that give them the distinctive, unique aura that makes them "Japanese."

It seems that by the beginning of the 21st century commercial designers in the United States had, in fact, begun to transcend their own cultural conditioning and their egos to produce designs that do, in fact, reflect *myo*—again primarily as a result of both competition and insight gained from right-brain created Japanese designs.

Bathing / *Suiyoku* [Sue-ee-yoh-kuu]
Historically, one of the weirdest aberrations of Christianity and other Western religions was associating

bathing with undesirable, if not sinful, sexual behavior and avoiding it except on rare occasions.

One of the first things Western missionaries did when they arrived in Japan in the mid-1500s, and again in the last half of the 1800s, was prohibit their converts from bathing every day—a practice that had been an integral part of Japanese culture since ancient times. When the missionaries realized how traumatic this ban was they relented to the point of allowing Japanese Christians to bathe a few times a month.

Obviously the Christian missionaries had no idea whatsoever of the spiritual importance of daily bathing to the Japanese. Shinto, the indigenous religion of the Japanese, taught that there were two forms of cleanliness—physical and spiritual—and that bathing daily cleansed both the body and the spirit.

The concept of spiritual cleansing with water was not unknown in the West. It was, in fact, common in Roman culture and in other ancient societies and did not become stigmatized for the majority of mankind until the appearance of Christianity and Islam.

But the Christian church did not wholly abandon the ancient connection between water and spiritual cleansing. It was kept as a part of the baptismal ceremony...by sprinkling water on babies and dunking adults in rivers.

The typical Westerner of today automatically associates bathing with getting ride of grime, sweat and body order—a strictly left-brain action—even though there is some awareness that a deep hot bath soothes the spirit as well as the body, and is often far more effective than praying in restoring the soul to equilibrium.

I recommend that Western cultures switch their left-brain concept of bathing to the right-brain, and reap both the physical and spiritual benefits that are provided by water.

Business Management / *Keiei* [Kay-eh-ee]

All of the aspects of Japan's traditional way of managing that are different from the Western way and responsible for most of the problems that develop between the Japanese and non-Japanese in business, in education, in politics and in all other affairs involving human interaction, are a direct result of the right-brain orientation of the Japanese and the left-brain orientation of non-Japanese.

In the simplest terms, these differences and problems arise because the non-Japanese tend to base their attitudes and behavior on linear thinking and reasoning, while the Japanese tend to think and behave in holistic and human terms.

There is a right-brain element in every custom, every practice, that defines the characteristic Japanese way of doing things. And by the same token, there is a left-brain element in all of the non-Japanese way of doing things. In some cases, the differences that arise from the right-brain and left-brain approaches are minor, and can generally be resolved fairly easily. In other cases, the two sides are simply too far apart to reach a compromise.

For their part, many of the Japanese involved in dealing with non-Japanese have become skilled to varying degrees in using the left side of their brains, particularly if they are using a foreign language. Hang-ups still occur among this group, however, because they are often not the final decision-makers in their companies, and still have to work in harmony with company members.

Native left-brain thinkers engaging in business and other affairs with the Japanese are generally less skilled in taking right-brain positions, and less inclined to do so when problems arise. Their normal reaction, usually automatic, is that their position is rational, reasonable and fair so altering their position wouldn't make sense.

Of course, the basic Japanese reaction is that their position is also the right one, and they rationalize and compromise their position only when they perceive that not doing so would result in a greater disadvantage. Given the various circumstances of Japan's position in relation to the rest of the world, the Japanese are more likely than non-Japanese to make compromises in order to create and sustain relationships.

Interestingly, there have been numerous situations in the past where the non-Japanese side held fast to their positions in the face of Japanese opposition, only to discover later that they would have been significantly better off if they had accepted the Japanese position.

When dealing with the Japanese, non-Japanese are advised to put their right-brain caps on and evaluate the situation from that side of their head before coming to final conclusions.

Bragging / *Jiman suru* [Jee-mahn sue-rue]

Bragging—characteristic of Americans—may seem to a left-brain person to be of small consequence, but it goes against the cultural grain of the Japanese, and is seen as both arrogant and uncultured, if not immoral.

The primary thrust of Japan's traditional culture was harmony first and last, and any kind of behavior that upset this harmony was seen as undesirable. Instead of bragging about their accomplishments or skills, it was characteristic of the Japanese to conceal them to avoid appearing conceited—and to be able to suddenly use them to catch people off guard and gain an advantage, or to surprise them and win their praise.

Bragging is still taboo as far as most Japanese are concerned, but there are growing numbers who are breaking this cultural mold because of new found courage and individuality—both of which are now approved of, in principle, by businesspeople, politicians and some bureaucrats.

Of course, the people in this latter category are generally the young and those who have been partially or completely de-Japanized by long-term exposure to Western, especially American, influences.

When contemplated by the left side of the brain, bragging is often a rational and reasonable thing to do, especially when the individual concerned can back up his or her claims by producing. It becomes immoral if it is intended to deceive.

Whether or not left-brain people should brag to the Japanese is therefore a moral judgment. The same rules should apply to the Japanese. Just as over-stating "facts" is immoral, concealing facts in order to gain an unfair advantage is also immoral.

One of the advantages that accrue to the Japanese as a result of their cultural taboo against bragging is that they are often underestimated and not taken as seriously as they should be, resulting in competitors and opponents lowering their guard and becoming more susceptible to being beaten.

Cute / *Kawaii* [Kah-wah-eee]

One of the more conspicuous elements in Japanese culture is what amounts to a virtual obsession with cuteness—individuals and things that are small, dainty and pretty. This compulsive attachment to cuteness especially applies to young girls, to small animals and to small objects, and is manifested widely in the culture—in toys, other products, printed advertisements, television commercials, cartoons and comics.

In the past, Westerners were inclined to view the attachment of adult Japanese to cuteness as a weakness, regarding it as immature if not infantile. This foreign attitude also tended to lead Westerners to underestimate the intellectual and physical abilities of the Japanese.

The accomplishments of the Japanese in the interim have pretty much eliminated this Western attitude, and now the Japanese penchant for building cuteness into things is being emulated in the West.

As it happened, there is a deep-seated part of the Western psyche that remembers the cuteness of infants and other small things, and now, with the success of the Japanese in merchandising cuteness so obvious, Westerners are not only allowing these emotions to surface, they are consciously making use of them.

So here again we have the right-brain orientation of the Japanese turning out to be a significant advantage in both product design and marketing.

Decision-Making / Kettei [Kay-ttay-ee]

Western businesspeople and diplomats who have encountered the Japanese way of making decisions might have some difficulty relating the process to positive aspects of their right-brain orientation, but a very good case can be made.

Two of the most common complaints that Westerners have traditionally lodged against their Japanese counterparts is the length of time it takes the Japanese to make decisions, and the fact that once they are made the Japanese do not necessarily treat them complete or as final.

The reason it takes the Japanese time to make most decisions is simple; they are made by consensus among many people, not by single individuals. By using the consensus approach to decisions, the Japanese are more likely to have the full support of everyone involved in whatever commitment is made.

As I have noted before there is a general belief in Japan that American businesspeople make decisions in a matter of hours if not minutes and then need a year or so to implement them; while the Japanese may take a year to make a decision but once the decision is made they implement it immediately.

The Japanese approach to decision-making incorporates the feelings and factual input from anywhere to a few to dozens of individuals, often contributing to both the quality of the decision and the chances that it will be carried out successfully.

This holistic approach to contemplating new ideas, new relationships, and decision-making has proven to be a major advantage for the Japanese. Just one example: the Japanese routinely involve product designers, engineers and assembly line experts in the process of creating new products, thereby avoiding many of the production and quality problems that so often plagued American manufacturers.

This is another example of Japan's human-oriented right-brain ingenuity that has since been copied by Westerners, including some American car manufacturers who finally began partially removing their corporate and cultural blinders in the late 1990s.

Etiquette / *Sahō* [Sah-hohh]

The Japanese have been famous for centuries for their highly stylized, virtually ritualized, system of etiquette. The right-brain orientation of the Japanese was certainly not exclusively responsible for the creation of this etiquette, but it had a great deal to do with its creation and its survival since ancient times.

The earliest day-to-day behavior of the Japanese was influenced by Shinto which incorporated paying highly formalized respect to the numerous gods that made up the Japanese pantheon. Between the 6th and 7th centuries, Japanese behavior was further influenced by the etiquette of Imperial China, with its respect forms of stylized behavior, titles, and wearing apparel.

Next came Japan's samurai class of warriors who ruled the country from 1192 until 1868. The code of ethics and etiquette that the samurai developed during this long reign—particularly from 1603 on—infused the culture of Japan with a form of etiquette that was as precise and as detailed as the behavior of actors on a stage.

Westerners who encountered Japanese during the early 1600s and again in the late 1800s were so impressed with the behavior of the average person they equated it with what one might expect of members of a royal court.

The traditional etiquette of the Japanese thus became a major asset that gave them a significant advantage in dealing with non-Japanese, especially Westerners whose manners were generally crude by comparison.

Still today Westerners in Japan are generally intimidated by the style and formality of Japanese etiquette, and generally go further than they normally do to avoid offending anyone. In this effort, it is common for Westerners to become less critical and more accommodating in their interactions with the Japanese, giving the Japanese an advantage.

Flattery / *Oseji* [Oh-say-jee]

In a society in which blunt comments and direct criticism were traditionally taboo and could get one shortened by a head the custom of *oseiji* [oh-say-jee], or flattery, not only became universal, it was developed into a fine art.

Flattery thus became one of the tools (or weapons!) that the Japanese consistently used in their dealings with others.

When the Japanese first began encountering Westerners it did not take them long to discover that they were especially susceptible to effusive praise, and that most of them—Americans in particular—could be manipulated like puppets.

The Japanese were and still are especially clever in the use of flattery because their right-brain orientation has made them extraordinarily experienced in dealing with, and playing on, human emotions.

Humility / *Kenkyo* [Kane-k'yoh]

The Japanese have always been among the proudest people on earth—at least in part because their creation myth says they were not just created by gods, but that they were the direct progeny of gods. [That's a lot more impressive than being made out of dirt and then infused with life!]

In any event, unbounded pride has been one of the primary characteristics of the Japanese since ancient times and has played a leading role in their history on an individual as well as a national basis.

This pride has manifested itself in a variety of ways in virtually every facet of Japanese culture and accomplishment—from the incredible skill the samurai achieved in swordsmanship, the level of mastery attained by artists and craftsmen, to today's success in the production of consumer and industrial goods.

What is remarkable about the pride of the Japanese, and what makes it quite different from the way of Americans and other Westerners is that in Japanese culture individually expressing pride or behaving in a prideful manner was taboo and regarded as a serious offense.

Humility, the exact opposite of prideful behavior, was seen as one of the prime virtues of humanity and the Japanese were conditioned to conduct themselves in a humble way, especially toward superiors.

Behaving in a humble manner is still characteristic of the Japanese, and commonly results in them gaining an advantage. Americans in particular appear to be psychologically programmed to go out of their way to help people who act in a humble manner.

Generally, Americans automatically equate humble behavior with lack of confidence, lack of experience, lack of ability, lack of knowledge, etc., and the tendency is for them to go out of their way to help such individuals.

The traditionally humble mode of the Japanese has probably got them more help from good-intentioned Americans than can be imagined—often without them asking for it. All the Japanese have to do to turn the typical American on is to act like they don't know what is going on.

Interestingly, the Japanese have the same psychological programming where non-Japanese are concerned, typically going out of their way to help foreign businesspeople [other than competitors] and visitors.

Still, in business situations the Japanese generally get more from Americans than what they give because the average American does not behave in a humble manner, and typically does not give the impression of needing help. But all they have to do is ask. This immediately puts the average Japanese in the help mode.

Mentoring in all areas of life is traditional among older Japanese, and they are especially programmed to help younger people. The humanistic influence of their right-brain orientation is primarily responsible for this trait.

Intelligence / *Chiryoku* [Chee-rio-kuu]

There are several kinds of intelligence, all generally recognized by people in all cultures. But the emphasis that cultures put on the different kinds of intelligence varies greatly. The Japanese have traditionally emphasized and developed their insight (intelligence) in human relations.

In effect, Japan's culture has traditionally given the highest priority to "emotional intelligence"—not book learning or the intelligence gained from practical experience. In earlier times the cultural and social standing of people was generally measured in terms of their emotional intelligence—their insight into human behavior and how to help themselves and others keep their emotions in balance.

Part of this emphasis on emotional balance came from their right-brain orientation. Another part came from the influence of Shinto and Buddhism, both of which emphasize physical, emotional and spiritual harmony.

Emotional intelligence continues to play a significant role in the Japanese penchant for working in groups, for resolving issues and making decisions by consensus, and for going out of their way to avoid disharmony.

Problems often arise, however, in their dealings with Westerners and others who do not give the same weight to emotional intelligence and in some cases ignore it altogether. The sensible recourse for the foreign side is, of course, to be aware of the role of emotional intelligence in Japanese life, and learn how to deal with it in an effective manner.

Mental Health / *Seishin no Kenkyō* [Say-sheen no Kane-k'yohh]

The cultural and social imperative of harmony in Japan's traditional society, which was both secular and spiritual in nature, made the Japanese especially sensitive to attitudes, moods and one's overall mental health.

This sensitivity played a fundamental role in the day-to-day etiquette that distinguished Japanese behavior, as well as in the creation and role of customs, or rituals if you will, that were designed to soothe the spirit, eliminate emotional turmoil and satisfy the intellect.

The most famous of these rituals was the tea ceremony. Other mass customs included flower-viewing, snow-viewing, writing poetry and communing with nature through gardens, mountains and woodlands.

Another national custom that was unique to Japan, in the sense that it was institutionalized as a cultural practice, was the holding of year-end parties called *bonenkai* (boh-nane-kigh), or "forget the year parties."

What was specifically unique to the *bonenkai*, which are still a common custom in Japan today, is that they were designed to help people rid themselves of any angry feelings that may have developed during the year against family members, co-workers and others.

This mass release of emotional grudges and hang-ups, a strictly right-brain function, contributes enormously to the mental health of the Japanese, and is a major factor in keeping the level of personal violence in Japan very low in comparison with the U.S. and other countries.

In other words, a combination of left-brain reasoning and right-brain wisdom resulted in the Japanese creating a cultural solution to psychological problems that are bound to arise among people—a factor that, until recent times, accounted for a very low incidence of psychiatric problems among the Japanese.

The rest of the world would be well-served by adopting and institutionalizing the Japanese custom of the *bonenkai*.

Problem Solving / *Nanmon* [Nahn-moan]

The Japanese are especially good at solving esoteric and technical problems, as is evidenced by their rapid adaptation of Western technology and their own technological innovations and discoveries after the Tokugawa Shogunate ended in 1868 and its virtual ban on change and research was eliminated.

While there had been almost no basic scientific research in Japan prior to the latter decades of the 19th century, the Japanese had been exposed to the highly sophisticated technology of the arts and crafts of China since the 6th century, and over the generations had made significant improvements in many of the manufacturing processes they learned from China.

Earthquake technology, for example, was highly developed in Japan by the time of the construction of the great Todai Temple in Nara in 724-749. Modern engineers who have been involved in maintenance on the building have been astounded by the construction techniques used to protect it from earthquakes. [It is said to be the largest wooden building in the world, and still today is an awesome sight.]

Throughout Japan's history the Japanese have not only been able to quickly understand any foreign technology that came their way, they invariably made improvements in it.

This impressive intellectual ability of the early Japanese no doubt had its roots in a combination of factors, including, once again, the right-brain orientation that resulted in them looking at things from all angles, being able to visualize them in various three-dimensional forms, and predict their behavior in these new forms.

A second factor in the intellectual prowess of the Japanese had to have been Zen Buddhism, which taught them to focus with laser-like intensity, and to use what might be called a "third eye" to grasp the inner workings of things.

A third factor that surely contributed to the problem-solving ability of the Japanese is their historical custom of working together in teams, traditionally in groups of five. If two heads are better than one, five heads are often better than two.

I believe that a fourth factor in the capacity of the Japanese to visualize intricate forms and recognize their relationship and coherency are the *Kanji* (Kahn-jee), the Chinese-created ideograms with which they write the core words of their language.

In early times, all educated Japanese learned how to read and draw at many as 5,000 of these ideograms, a process that trained the eye, the mind, and the hand to see small intricate forms clearly and to duplicate them with considerable skill.

Present-day Japanese students are required to learn only 1,945 Kanji, and many of them soon forget some of the more complicated forms after they leave school.

But learning even this comparatively small number has a discernible, positive influence on the Japanese.

Self-Respect & Pride / *Jichō* [Jee-chohh] / *Jiman* [Jee-man]

One of the traditional characteristics of the Japanese was an extraordinarily strong sense of self-respect as individuals and an equally powerful sense of pride as members of certain groups and as Japanese

The exceptional sense of self-respect that distinguished the Japanese evolved out of the very high standards of behavior set by their culture and the social system under which they had lived since ancient times.

Self-respect could only be earned by successfully conforming to all of the demands of the culture and social system. In other words, Japanese style self-respect was not based on individual knowledge, skills, accomplishments or feelings of self-worth. It was based on behaving in the prescribed and expected manner, which included working hard and diligently and being scrupulously honest.

The social system required the Japanese to think and behave as members of groups. With few if any exceptions, behaving as individuals on the basis of self-interest was regarded as anti-social and anti-Japanese. Even self-employed artists and craftsmen had to conform to a variety of customs and rules to avoid being ostracized.

Likewise, the extraordinary pride of the Japanese was not an individualized thing. It was based on the shared culture and on all of the accomplishments of the past—on the Japanese concept of themselves as members of an extraordinary race, as the creators of an extraordinary culture, and as a people with a spirit that set them apart from all others.

While events in modern times have dramatically changed the Japanese view of themselves, making them far less ethnocentric, they continue to be motivated by a strong sense of self-respect and pride that is reflected in their economic success and in their growing role in international affairs—all fueled by contributions from their right-brain orientation.

Sex / *Sei* [Say]

One of the most important factors in Japan's traditional culture came from the very core of Shintoism—which is essentially nature worship based on fertility.

Many of the Shintō gods of Japan (there were eight million of them!) were specifically concerned with fertility, which in human terms means sex. But rather than repress the sexual impulse and make it a sin, Japan's gods celebrated it.

The Japanese were wise enough to understand that people need to engage in sex regularly in order to remain physically, emotionally and spiritually healthy. They were thus spared the agony and suffering that has been afflicted upon Christian, Hebrew and Islamic societies by their male religious leaders who took the opposite view.

It may be a stretch to some to say that one of the reasons the Japanese are a superior people is because they did not turn sex into a sin and make its repression one of the most destructive forces ever unleashed on humanity.

Still today religious leaders and their followers are ignorant of or ignore the fact that sexual repression is the source of much of the violence that afflicts mankind.

In any event, the fact that Japan avoided being Christianized contributed immeasurably to its survival and its subsequent economic success.

Shame / *Haji* [Hah-jee]

As mentioned earlier, the right-brain orientation of the Japanese led them to be extraordinarily conscious of and sensitive to the behavior of others, resulting in them developing a "shame culture" rather than the kind of "guilt culture" that is characteristic of Christian, Jewish and Islamic societies.

Japanese behavior has never been controlled by internal feelings of guilt and fear of punishment by some unseen, all-powerful god. Their behavior has been controlled by feelings of shame that resulted if they did not conform to precise standards of etiquette and behavior that were visible for all to see or hear, whether or not that behavior contravened secular law.

The Japanese not only punish themselves by experiencing strong feelings of shame when they do something society regards as wrong, they are also subject to a variety of sanctions by others around them, adding to their sense of shame.

Since the first punishment for misbehaving in a shame culture is self-inflicted and immediate, shame is generally more effective in controlling the behavior of people than spiritual-oriented guilt feelings, which can be downplayed or denied altogether.

While Shinto and Confucianism provided much of the foundation and framework of Japan's shame culture, the emotional content deriving from the right-brain orientation of the people no doubt added enormously to its power to motivate and control them.

Spirituality / *Seishinteki* [Say-sheen-tay-kee] / *Tōshi* [Tohh-she]

The Japanese have never been religious in the Western sense of the term. But until modern times they were among the most spiritual of all people. They regularly followed precise customs and rituals to keep themselves in harmony with nature and the spirit world.

Today, the spiritual foundation of Japanese culture has been pushed into the background but it is still there in the hearts of the older generations and is still acknowledged on special occasions by the young. And there are signs that more and more Japanese are rediscovering the importance of the spiritual side of life—not as preached or practiced in the organized religions of the world, but as a part of their traditional culture.

Some of the spiritual wisdom that a growing number of Japanese are returning to is found in Shintō, their ancient indigenous "religion," which has been pushed into the background by the popular culture of the West, but it is still there in the subconscious of the people, waiting to be revived.

The ancient Japanese, like other ancient people, understood the physical and spiritual relationship between man, the Earth and the cosmos far better than those whose view of the world and man's place in it became distorted beyond reason by Judaism, Christianity and Islam.

A full-fledged revival of the positive elements of Shintō would put the Japanese ahead of much of the rest of the world in spiritual terms, and provide an example for the people worldwide.

Organized religions of the West and Near East are, in fact, gradually disappearing and being replaced by individual efforts to connect with the spiritual dimension of life and the cosmos. The more educated people become in the societies dominated by Christianity, Judaism and Islam, and the more individual freedom they achieve, the more rapidly these religions will become irrelevant.

Style / *Katachi* [Kah-tah-chee] / *Sŭtairu* [Suu-tie-rue]

The right-brain orientation of the Japanese, and the resulting feminine orientation of Japanese culture, have made the Japanese especially style-conscious and provided them with the ability to create refined, pleasing forms and styles.

This mind-set and ability applies across the board in all areas of Japanese life, and is especially conspicuous in the arts, crafts, interior decorations, house wares, and more—including such mundane things as wrapping paper and shopping bags.

The style of Japanese things is distinguished by their aesthetic appeal and by a sensuality that derives from their form, the materials used and the harmonious use of colors and decorations. A lacquered jewelry box, for example, that combines the richness of black lacquer flaked with silver and gold has a beauty that transcends the materials it is made from.

By using the left side of their brains to conceive of articles that have practical, commercial value, and then bringing the right side of their brains into play in the designing and finishing of the product, the Japanese are able to create products that are both beautiful and saleable.

In the 1990s some American and other Western designers began to pick up on and use *Elements of Japanese Design* [the title of one of my books!], dramatically increasing the aesthetically qualities, user friendliness, and functionality of their products.

*

Failing the Test for Quality

One of the aspects of the Japanese obsession with quality is that it covers the whole product, including areas that are not ordinarily seen—the bottom, inside and so on. Many Western products have failed the Japanese test for quality because they were not fully finished or detailed.
Despite fundamental cultural changes among Japan's younger generations they generally remain among the world's most discrimination consumers.
American manufacturers wanting to sell consumer merchandise in the Japanese market would be wise to keep this factor in mind.

*

*

In Japan Things Work!

If you ask long-term foreign residents of Japan what they find most impressive about the country [besides the sensual nature of the culture and the character of the people] they almost always add "The fact that everything works!"

Japan's trains, both commuter and long-distance "Bullet Trains," are among the most amazing examples of efficiency in Japan. If a "Bullet Train" is more than a few seconds late in arriving and departing there is an inquiry and steps are taken to remedy whatever caused the delay. If a train is going to be as much as 15 or 20 seconds late at a station an announcement and an apology are broadcast over a PA system.

*

[END]

WHY THE JAPANESE ARE A SUPERIOR PEOPLE!

LaVergne, TN USA
05 December 2010
207467LV00007B/120/P